Lost Mines *and*
Buried Treasures
of Arizona

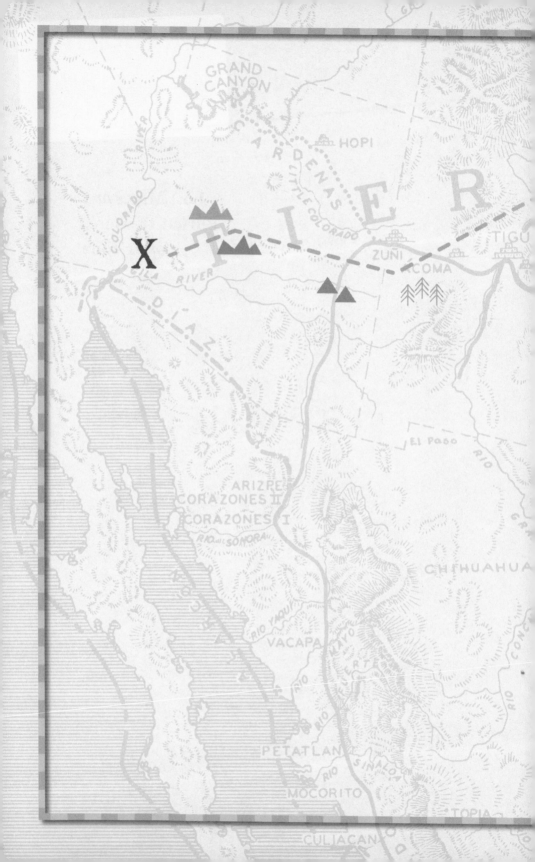

Lost Mines and Buried Treasures of Arizona

W. C. JAMESON

UNIVERSITY OF NEW MEXICO PRESS | ALBUQUERQUE

© 2009 by the University of New Mexico Press
All rights reserved. Published 2009
Printed in the United States of America

14   13   12   11   10   09   1   2   3   4   5   6

Library of Congress Cataloging-in-Publication Data
Jameson, W. C., 1942–
  Lost mines and buried treasures of Arizona / W.C. Jameson. — 1st ed.
     p. cm.
ISBN 978-0-8263-4413-7 (pbk. : alk. paper)
1. Arizona—History, Local—Anecdotes. 2. Treasure troves—Arizona—
Anecdotes. 3. Arizona—Antiquities—Anecdotes. 4. Gold mines and
mining—Arizona—History—Anecdotes. 5. Silver mines and mining—
Arizona—History—Anecdotes. 6. Outlaws—Arizona—History—
Anecdotes. 7. Legends—Arizona. I. Title.
F811.6.J36 2009
398.2709791—dc22

2008048168

Book design and type composition by Melissa Tandysh
Composed in 11/13.75 Minion Pro
Display type is ITC Goudy Sans
Map: *Coronado and His Contemporaries*, drawn by Constant F. Davis,
     compiled by Herbert Bolton

Contents

Introduction

Arizona is a remarkable place for myriad reasons. This Southwestern state is the setting for bustling cities, colorful small towns, and a number of historic ghost towns. It is also the home to some of the most spectacular landscapes in the United States, including the Grand Canyon, Petrified Forest, and the saguaro-studded Sonoran Desert. Arizona also contains remote and forbidding wilderness, and environments ranging from snow-capped peaks to arid desert.

Many know Arizona as a favorite Western vacation destination. Scratch the surface of the commercial side of the Grand Canyon State, however, and uncover a country rich in history, culture, geology, flora, and fauna, as well as a source of compelling legend and lore, particularly about lost mines and buried treasures.

The Land

Mention Arizona to geologists and their eyes will light up with thoughts of igneous, sedimentary, and metamorphic landscapes that served as settings for important geomorphic events of eons gone by. Arizona is replete with long-dormant volcanoes, evidence of a turbulent geologic past. Long ago, volcanoes spilled lava and ash onto the Arizona crust, giving shape and texture to the state we know today. Unseen, however, was the molten magma that never escaped from the depths to extrude onto the *terra firma* to cool and give rise to vast lava beds. Some of the superheated fluid rock was forced into deep faults and fissures, where it was trapped and cooled slowly hundreds and thousands of feet below the surface. In these closed environments, precious metals such as gold and silver were formed over time. These sometimes extensive pockets and seams of gold and silver, as well as other important minerals, resided unseen for ages until such time as they were eventually exposed. Strong earthquakes were in large part responsible for revealing much of this valuable material at the surface; portions of the earth's crust were folded, fractured, and heaved upward, their fault scarps sometimes exhibiting outcrops and seams of ore. Some of these exposed veins were encountered by the early Spanish explorers during the sixteenth and seventeenth centuries, and led to the development of some of the richest mines in the history of the United States. Many Western locations lay claim to being the home of the "biggest" or "richest" mine, but the simple truth is that the state of Arizona can contend with any and all of them for wealth dug from the earth.

The People

The first to locate and extract ore from the native rock were the indigenous peoples who originally settled the region. The numerous Indian tribes—Apache, Hopi, Navajo, Papago, Pima, Ute, Zuni, and others—had little use for gold or silver save for the fashioning of ornaments such as bracelets, armbands, necklaces, and earrings. After the arrival of the Europeans, the tribes learned that they could trade ore for foodstuffs and supplies as well as for arms and ammunition. The mining of the ore by the indigenes was rare and had a minimal impact on the landscape.

During the sixteenth century, the Spanish arrived. These newcomers from across the Atlantic Ocean were given a mission by their political and religious leaders to explore the new lands in the Western Hemisphere and assess the potential for settlement, commerce, ranching, farming, and mining. In the process, they were to convert the natives to Christianity. It was not unusual for a Spanish exploration team to include not only soldiers, but mining engineers, geologists, administrators, and priests.

That the Spaniards found gold and silver in abundance in the new land called Arizona is well documented. Indeed, hundreds of mines were opened, and untold millions of dollars worth of ore was dug from the ground. The Indians, in the process of being converted, were often enslaved to work in the deepening shafts. They were chained together at the neck, provided with poor rations and housing, and forced to labor as long as eighteen hours a day. Many died in their chains, others starved to death, and some were killed because their production did not meet expectations. The greatest portion of the gold and silver taken from these Arizona mines was at the expense of hundreds of lives. The ore, refined and molded into ingots, was transported via pack train to Mexico City. From there, it was taken to the east coast of Mexico, loaded onto ships, and delivered to the treasury in Spain. The wealth remaining in Mexico was often used by the church to sustain their efforts in Christianizing the New World heathens.

Spain was on its way to becoming the richest nation in the world as it amassed great fortunes of gold and silver. Then came the decree from King Charles III in 1767 expelling all Jesuits from Spain and its possessions. As a result, the mines, many of them still rich and productive, were closed down, sealed up, and abandoned. Mine administrators and engineers presumed there would come a day when they would be able to return to these environs to renew their quest for gold and silver, but that day never came. When the Spanish departed the region, they carried with them documents and maps describing the locations of the mines and their productivity. Many of the documents were lost, but to date dozens have been found in archives in Mexico City and in Spain.

After the Spanish departed the region, a number of Mexican mining expeditions traveled north. Some of them, possessing information obtained from Spanish records, reopened a few of the original mines. Others discovered new sources of gold and silver and dug new shafts. The Indians, recalling the dark days of enslavement by the previous miners, waged war on the newcomers.

In 1848, gold in abundance was discovered at Sutter's Mill, California. After word of the discovery spread across the country, tens of thousands of hopeful fortune seekers from the American East and South traveled to the Golden State with hopes and dreams of becoming rich. Many failed; but on return trips, some lingered in Arizona long enough to find deposits of gold and silver, thus forming the beginnings of the many mining empires that evolved.

Time and again, stories were told of a major discovery in some distant range of mountains of Arizona. The finder, usually some prospector wandering the countryside on his own, would travel to the nearest town, acquire a grubstake to get outfitted, and then attempt to return to the claim, only to become confused and lost. Many forgotten mines reside in the remote canyons and mountain ranges throughout the state.

Early on, some decided that digging for ore was far too much work, that it was easier to simply steal the precious metal from stagecoaches and trains. Outlaws flocked into Arizona, drawn by the promise of the easy robbery of gold and silver from the mining and transportation companies. Dozens, if not hundreds, of coach and train robberies took place during the heyday of mining and shipping ore during the late 1800s. Many outlaws, however, never got to spend their newly acquired wealth. They were forced to abandon their booty during the pursuit by lawmen and railroad authorities. In subsequent shootouts, the robbers were often killed, leaving none left to reveal where the treasure was hidden. Such caches are a matter of record, and many are still being searched for today.

From such origins as the above, as well as others, come uncountable tales and legends of lost mines and buried treasures throughout much of Arizona. The state is rich in such history and folklore. Many consider it the most promising location in the United States to search for riches long forgotten or lost.

Legend and Lore

Since the beginning of recorded history, tales and legends of hidden treasures and lost mines have held a strange fascination for people. Reading about a quest for a lost mine or a long-buried treasure excites men and women, young and old, and the attraction has not lessened since the times of Jason and the Argonauts and their quest for the Golden Fleece. Readers continue to remain spellbound by the tales of King Solomon's Mines, by the lure of sunken treasures just off the eastern and western coasts of America, and by the Lost Dutchman Mine of the Superstition Mountains of Arizona. Ask people in the United States to identify a famous lost mine and they will almost always respond with the Lost Dutchman.

The tales contained in this book represent some of the most compelling to originate in Arizona. The majority of these stories have been handed down through generations via the oral tradition. Many, such as the Lost Dutchman Mine, are part of the historical record. In the retelling of the stories, facts are sometimes exaggerated, misrepresented, omitted, or forgotten. Where this was suspected during the compilation of the material for this book, attempts were made to authenticate the tales, at least as much as one can validate folklore. Others are better documented, and have been gleaned from more than forty years of research and collection of materials, letter writing, and prowling the remote corners and dark aisles of Arizona's libraries to examine old journals and diaries. Countless hours have been spent searching for and exploring the locations of lost mines and buried treasures mentioned in this book.

Tales of lost mines and buried treasures are a product of the land and the people. The rich variety of landscapes and cultures found in Arizona are significant to the generating of such stories. And the stories cut across all cultures—Indian, Spanish, Mexican, and white settlers, soldiers, miners, lawmen, and others. The nature of these tales is as old as storytelling itself. They involve the quest for treasure and the overcoming of obstacles in order to possess the object of the search. Lost or hidden treasure has been found in Arizona. In my own explorations, I have found some.

On occasion I was rewarded by my research and site search for a particular lost treasure. I never grew wealthy, but I came away better off than when I started. I managed to pay off bills, close the notes for a couple of houses and vehicles, and send my children to college. I did, however, accumulate a fortune of a different sort. I had the good luck to become acquainted with many tales of lost and cached treasure, some large, some small. These folkloric treasures possess immeasurable value, as they are products of the culture and the land. I also amassed the wealth of getting to know people who have spent their lifetimes searching for one particular treasure or another. I listened to them speak of their dreams. It occurred to me that such folk were today's Argonauts, the wealth seekers of legend. From them I learned about hope and endurance, about character and determination.

I came away from these experiences with a deep appreciation for Arizona: the people, the places, the history, the culture. And I continue to remain impressed by the legacy of lore and legend as it relates to lost mines and buried treasures. My interest, as well as my research, continues, as the does the search for lost treasure.

I return to Arizona on a regular basis, still searching, still exploring—not only for the gold and silver that awaits the persistent and fortunate searcher. I am still discovering. More and more, I return to be involved in this process, as well as to learn. In so doing I encounter rewards. Sometimes I return with an ingot or two of gold or silver; sometimes the discovery is of a new tale. In either case, I always return a wealthier man.

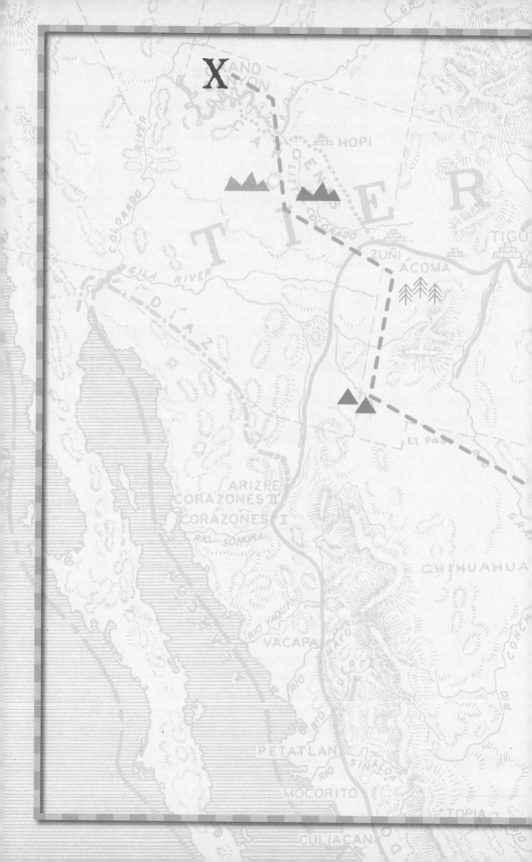

Northwest

The Ranch Hand's Secret Gold Mine

He was known only as Ben, and that may not have been his real name. Whatever his last name, he never gave it. Ben was a loyal employee of Major Abraham Peeples, an Arizona entrepreneur, miner, rancher, and investor. Peeples Valley, a small community thirty miles southwest of Prescott, is named for him. Ben served as Peeples's ranch foreman for many years. With the help of an area Indian he befriended, Ben located a rich deposit of gold, which he harvested from time to time. Ben died without revealing the location.

During his lifetime, Major Abraham Peeples experienced far more success than the average man, and each of his successes seemed to lead to another. In 1863, Peeples was prospecting for precious metals in the mountains found in present-day La Paz County. Now and then he found traces of gold, but never enough to justify launching a major mining operation. The country in which Peeples and other miners prospected was home to Apache Indians who posed a continuous threat to the whites.

Not all of the Indians were hostile. From time to time, a young Apache would arrive at Peeples's camp in need of supplies such as coffee or sugar. Initially, Peeples shared what he had, and the Indian offered thanks and departed. During one visit after Peeples had offered some coffee and flour, the Apache offered to pay him. He presented Peeples with a handful of gold. After several more visits, Peeples realized he took in more gold from the Indian than he had been digging out of the ground.

Late one afternoon when the young Apache came to Peeples's camp, the miner fed him a large meal and plied him with questions about the origin of the gold. The Indian pointed vaguely toward a low range of mountains east of the small village of La Paz, now a ghost town. He told Peeples there was more gold there than ten men could carry away in a year. Intrigued, Peeples proposed a bargain. If the Apache would agree to lead Peeples and a small party of miners to the source of the gold, he would be allowed to select four mules from Peeples's remuda. Since mules were more prized by the Indians than gold, the Apache agreed.

Days later, Peeples gathered five or six miners, including a black man named Ben. Following the Indian, they were led into the La Paz Mountains. On the third day, they stood atop a low hill. The Indian pointed to the ground. It was covered with gold nuggets. The location became known as Rich Hill, and it is estimated that over twenty million dollars worth of gold was taken from it.

Peeples invested in other mining adventures, each of which yielded additional fortunes. In each case, he appointed Ben as supervisor of operations. Ben was a loyal and competent employee, and Peeples paid him well. The only problem the major ever had with Ben had to do with drinking. Ben had a weakness for whiskey, and it often got the better of him.

Eventually, tiring of living and working in harsh and sometimes dangerous environments, as well as having to live under the threat of warring Apaches, Peeples purchased a ranch southwest of Prescott and retired to it. He appointed Ben as his ranch foreman. Area residents called it Peeples Valley.

Over time, Ben developed a friendship with an elderly Apache who had been hanging around the ranch. Once in a while Ben would give him a job, but the old man was too infirm to do much. One evening, seated around a campfire following a day of stringing fence on a remote part of the ranch, the two men ate their supper, drank coffee, and exchanged conversation. In this manner, Ben learned of another rich gold deposit, one known only to the Apaches.

Time passed, and Ben took to drinking more. It was said that after he got paid, he would ride to Prescott and spend his entire paycheck on whiskey. When he sobered up and returned to the ranch days later, he was broke and forced to do without drink until the next payday. The wait became too much for him.

One afternoon, Ben located the old Apache and asked him questions about the gold. The Indian told Ben that he was forbidden by his tribe to reveal the location. Ben persisted, however, saying he only wanted a little of the precious metal so he could buy whiskey. He promised the old man

W. C. JAMESON

he would share it with him. Weeks later the old man relented and agreed to lead Ben to the gold. Once or twice a month thereafter, Ben would ride to the secret location, harvest a few nuggets, and return. Though Ben stayed drunk more often, Peeples tolerated his foreman.

When Ben started paying for his whiskey with gold nuggets, some of his fellow drinkers grew curious and asked questions about the source. The ranch hand remained silent, keeping a promise to the Indian that he would never tell anyone. On occasion, he noted men following him when he rode out to get more gold. He devised a number of schemes for eluding his trackers, and always made it to the source and back without being detected.

More and more people in Prescott became interested in the source of Ben's gold. He knew he was followed every time he rode out of town. Though no one ever tracked him to the gold, those who trailed him all reported that he entered the Harquahala Mountains, located about forty miles southwest of the ranch. On his return trips, his pockets filled with gold, he was seen leaving the same range. While he never allowed any of his trackers to follow him to the gold, he was warned many times by the old Indian to never allow the Apaches to observe him taking the metal. If he did, he would surely be killed.

After several years of taking gold from the Harquahala range, Ben was found dead on the road a few miles west of Wickenburg. He was apparently on his way back to the ranch, and his pockets were filled with nuggets of almost pure gold. Evidence at the site suggested he had been attacked and slain by Apaches.

On learning of Ben's trips to the Harquahalas to harvest gold, Major Peeples grew curious about the size of the deposit. Soon he was over-taken by a fever to locate the ore and establish a mine. Initiating a search based on what he learned from Prescott citizens, Peeples entered the Harquahala Mountains in search of what he called Ben's Lost Gold Mine. Peeples spent the rest of his life searching for it, unsuccessfully.

Few people alive today know the story of Ben and his gold. As a result, there has been little or no activity related to undertaking a search into the Harquahalas. From time to time, a hunter or hiker will come out of the range and show friends some colorful ore they chanced upon. When later informed it was gold, some have attempted to retrace their route, all to no avail.

The gold—Ben's gold—is still there.

Waterfall
Gold

Deep in the Grand Canyon of the Colorado River can be found hundreds of smaller gorges that intersect with the main stream. At certain locations where varieties of igneous intrusive rock have been exposed from the easily eroded sandstone and other sediments that dominate the canyon, gold has been found. Some distance west of Tanner Trail in the canyon is a slope where, according to one source, nuggets lie on the ground in abundance. During the latter part of the nineteenth century, these were harvested with ease by a man whose identity remains a mystery. A description of the location, along with a map and a letter detailing his discovery and subsequent tragedy, were discovered in 1910 and led a second man to the site. He, in turn, found the gold, but experienced hardship and was able to retrieve only a handful of the ore. He passed away without ever returning to the site or leaving pertinent directions. The location continues to baffle treasure hunters today.

During the winter of 1910, Tom Watson arrived in Flagstaff, Arizona, some seventy-five straight-line miles south of the Grand Canyon, and moved into an abandoned cabin. Little was known about Watson except that he was a solitary prospector who ranged in the area of the Grand Canyon in search of precious metals and stones. He remained in and near the canyon until the first snows struck; then he would retreat southward and winter in Flagstaff.

After taking over the old cabin, Watson set about cleaning the place of pack-rat nests and other debris, a chore that took several days. While engaged in the task of making the cabin livable, Watson found several boxes of old newspapers, catalogs, and letters. He swept these aside, believing they would be useful for starting fires in the cast-iron wood-stove on cold mornings.

Several weeks after moving in, Watson loaded the stove with kindling and picked up a handful of the letters to use to light a fire. As he poked them under the wood, he noticed an envelope that had never been opened. Curious, he set it aside and worked at building a blaze and making coffee.

Later, he retrieved and examined the envelope. The name and address, written in blue ink, had become wet and smeared, making it illegible. Watson slit open the envelope and withdrew the letter. Folded within was a piece of brown wrapping paper upon which a map had been sketched. Setting the map aside, Watson read the letter. What he learned filled him with excitement and wonder.

The letter, dated May 28, 1904, and addressed "Dear Brother" with no name provided, went on to explain that whoever wrote the missive had been carried to this cabin to recover from gunshot wounds suffered during an attack somewhere deep in the Grand Canyon.

"I found the ground covered with gold nuggets," the letter said, "and filled an ore sack preparatory to coming out. That night, two men I had suspected of following me rode into camp."

Fearing that the newcomers might rob him, the letter writer made some excuse to leave camp for a few minutes. After retrieving his sackful of gold from his saddlebags, he made his way to a nearby waterfall he described as being twenty-two feet high. Noticing a small cave behind the falls, he threw his sack into it through the falling water. Should his visitors prove harmless, he reasoned, he could retrieve the gold in the morning.

As he made his way back to camp, he found the two men going though his belongings and removing items from his tent. He hollered at them and they responded by pulling their revolvers and opening fire. During the ensuing gunfight, he wounded one of them and succeeded in driving them off, but in the process received two bullets himself. Weak and in pain, he crawled to his burro, pulled himself onto it, and attempted to ride out of the canyon. Hours later he fell from the back of the animal and lay unconscious.

The next morning he was discovered by two government surveyors, who carried him out of the canyon and to a doctor. The doctor pronounced his condition critical and had him transported to his cabin in Williams, thirty miles west of Flagstaff. There, the prospector penned the letter to his brother in Flagstaff, providing directions to the waterfall. He drew the map on a piece of brown wrapping paper. The letter arrived in Flagstaff, but for whatever reason, was never opened.

Watson pondered his discovery. He was somewhat familiar with the part of the Grand Canyon described by the prospector and believed, given enough time and some luck, he could find the waterfall. He asked questions around Flagstaff, seeking to learn the identity of the prospector or his brother, but was unsuccessful. He traveled by train to Williams in search of clues. Eventually, he encountered a Dr. Rounseville who told Watson he recalled treating a prospector years before. The man, he said, had two bullet wounds. As the doctor recalled, the prospector died a week later and was buried in an unmarked grave in the cemetery. The man had not provided the doctor with his name, and no one in the area was acquainted with him.

Watson returned to Flagstaff to await the onset of spring. When warmer weather finally arrived, he outfitted himself, loaded his mule, and made the journey to Havasupai Canyon. Watson had a hunch the waterfall could be found in a small canyon that intersected Havasupai. On arriving, he realized the map was less than specific, and contained lines representing a number of small canyons all emptying into Havasu Creek, the stream that flowed through the bottom of the larger canyon.

Watson searched from April through October of 1911 and found nothing. As winter moved in, he decided that the map did indeed represent the Grand Canyon and not Havasupai. He returned to Flagstaff determined to try again in 1912.

After several weeks of searching in April and May, Watson was forced to abandon the project in order to return to Flagstaff and renew his supplies. He spoke with two men who were somewhat familiar with the Grand Canyon. They told him waterfalls were numerous in the side canyons, but were normally only active during the snowmelt of early spring. The rest of the time, the falls were merely dry ledges.

Watson returned to the Grand Canyon. From the point where Havasu Creek joined the Colorado River, he explored upstream. He now believed the place he was looking for was located between that point and the junction with the Little Colorado River, about 120 miles upstream. Watson searched diligently, stopping only long enough to resupply.

By June 1914, Watson was growing discouraged, but he persevered. One morning he was following what was known locally as the Horse

Thief Trail, but the government maps labeled it Tanner Trail. He followed it eastward, descending from the base of Moran Point and crossing the river. Around noon, thinking of stopping long enough to prepare something to eat, he heard the sound of falling water. Curious, he rode his mule about two hundred yards up a nearby gorge and found a waterfall. Watson dismounted and climbed up the rest of the rocky slope on foot. As he neared the fall, he estimated it to be about twenty-two feet high and about ten feet wide, but he could not tell for certain whether or not there was a cave behind it.

Watson sat upon a rock and surveyed the site. He was unable to reach the area behind the waterfall from where he sat, so he approached it from the opposite side. From there he could peer behind the falling water, where he spotted a cave. Proceeding with caution from the slippery rock wall to which he clung, Watson inched his way along a narrow ledge about fifteen feet above the pool at the bottom. From the ledge he jumped into the cave, landing on the rocky floor of a dark, cool recessed area.

From his shirt pocket he withdrew a match, struck it, and held it just above the floor of the cave. There, glittering in the light, he saw a scattering of gold nuggets. He picked one up, examined it closely, and determined it was a high grade of gold. After lighting five matches and inventorying the floor of the cave, Watson estimated that there were enough nuggets to fill a bushel basket. Watson figured that rodents had gnawed the ore sack until there was nothing left and scattered the contents. Here and there, scraps of the cloth could be found.

Watson decided he would lead his mule as close to the waterfall as possible. From his pack he would retrieve a few empty cotton ore sacks, return to the cave, and fill them with the gold. One by one he would carry them out, pack them onto the mule, and leave for Flagstaff. By this time next month, Watson told himself, he would be a rich man. Before leaving the cave, Watson placed four of the biggest gold nuggets into a hip pocket.

From the edge of the cave, Watson leaped back onto the ledge. His slick-soled boots did not afford him a purchase on landing, and his feet shot out from under him. He struggled to obtain a handhold. Seconds later he plummeted downward into the pool of water below. Minutes later, Watson lay gasping on the lower edge of the pool, his body half in the water. In pain, it took him several minutes to realize his left shinbone was broken. As he regained his composure, he contented himself with the fact that he had found the gold hidden behind the waterfall. According to the letter, there was more gold to be found on a nearby slope. Indeed, he repeated to himself, he would be a wealthy man. But first, he had to get out of the canyon and get treatment for his broken leg.

In great pain, Watson crawled out of the pool and down the slope to where he had left his mule. It took him all evening and most of the night. By the time he reached the animal, the sky was growing light. After resting, Watson withdrew a hatchet from one of the saddlebags and hacked a pair of splints from a nearby juniper. Before attaching the splints to his calf, he withdrew his boot and found a half-dozen pea-sized nuggets within, gold he must have picked up as he made his way down the slope. This must have been the slope, he concluded, from which the letter writer found his gold.

With great effort, Watson managed to climb atop his mule and guide the animal out of the gorge and back into the canyon. For hours he returned along Tanner Trail, eventually arriving at the Martin Buggelin ranch near the south rim.

Rancher Buggelin treated Watson's broken leg as best he could. He loaded the prospector into a wagon and hauled him to the lumber-mill physician at Flagstaff. By now, gangrene had set in and Watson was in danger of dying. The doctor's treatment, coupled with Watson's determination to live, pulled him through the worst of the infection. It was four months before Watson could walk again.

Watson sold some of his nuggets to pay the doctor and to purchase supplies for a return trip to the waterfall. During the fall of 1914, Watson, riding his mule and pulling a burro laden with supplies and equipment, returned to the Grand Canyon. His dreams of wealth had never left him. He was more determined than ever to retrieve the gold behind the waterfall and along the slope.

Fortune abandoned Watson. Though he searched for months, he was never able to relocate the same waterfall. He returned to Flagstaff and told his tale to a veterinarian named Roy Scanlon. Scanlon became intrigued by Watson's discovery and offered to go along and help him search. Together the two men returned to the canyon during the winter of 1915. It snowed most of the time they searched, and Watson insisted that the snow cover confused him and prevented him from locating specific landmarks. They searched until midspring and finally acknowledged defeat.

W. C. JAMESON

After resting himself and his animals for a month, Watson returned for another search. He stayed out for two months, all for naught. He left the canyon and, following the Grand Canyon–Flagstaff stagecoach road, pulled off the trail and set up camp for the night at Deadman Flat.

Alone and depressed, Watson must have considered the great fortune he had found and lost—considered that he would never realize his dreams. He leaned back against a tree and placed the stock of his .30-30 Winchester between his feet and the barrel in his mouth. Using a stick to reach the trigger, he ended his disappointment.

Watson was found two days later. In his pockets were two of the large gold nuggets he had retrieved from the cave behind the waterfall.

Zuni
Gold

Jim White, traveling on a crude, homemade raft of cottonwood logs, floated down 550 miles of the Colorado River in 1867. Though Major John Wesley Powell is given credit for being the first to do so, White beat him by two years and was belatedly recognized for his efforts. Since Powell had more friends and connections in the government than White, a monument was erected honoring him for the feat. In 1917, White was finally recognized by Congress as the first man to travel the Colorado River.

While undertaking his momentous journey down the Colorado River, White encountered life-threatening hazards. His sole companion was swept away in the mighty current and drowned. At one point during the terrifying voyage, White, in attempting to climb out of the canyon, chanced upon an ancient Zuni Indian cache of gold nuggets. He was unable to carry the gold away. The fortune, worth millions of dollars today, still lies in a remote cave deep in the rugged fastness of the Grand Canyon.

Jim White traveled into Arizona in 1865 from his hometown of Kenosha, Wisconsin. Like many during that time, he came west to try to find his fortune prospecting for gold and silver in the rocky outcrops of northern Arizona. Experiencing one failure after another in the Four Corners region of Arizona, Utah, Colorado, and New Mexico, White decided to head to California in search of better luck. Possessing neither money nor horses, White, along with friends Ben Dunlap and George Strole, traveled on foot across the rocky desert of northern Arizona. During their trip, they met Captain James Baker. Baker was evasive about his

18

background, and his rank of captain may have been self-bestowed. In any case, Baker proved to be a source of difficulties for the small party.

After several days of walking, Baker suggested they steal some horses from the next village of Ute Indians they encountered. One night, the four men entered a brush corral a short distance from a Ute camp and made off with four horses. They fled, following the Mancos River into New Mexico.

Luck was not with them. The following morning they were overtaken by some Utes in pursuit, several of them armed with rifles. In the first few seconds, Baker was shot dead by a fusillade of bullets. Moments later Dunlap fell, never to rise again.

White and Strole spurred their mounts hard and were soon out of range of the Utes' rifles. They rode until their horses could go no farther, finally stopping in a box canyon. Fearing that the Indians knew the country better than they, they turned the horses loose and proceeded on foot. They counted on the Indians being satisfied just to recover the stolen horses. They hoped the Indians would terminate their pursuit.

For two days the men traveled on foot before arriving at another, much larger canyon. At the bottom ran a fast-moving river. White and Strole had no notion that they had arrived at the Grand Canyon of the Colorado River. While camped in a grove of cottonwood trees at the bottom of the gorge, White decided their only means of escape would be to construct a raft and float down the stream. In their packs, each man carried a small amount of food, a pistol, some ropes, and a hatchet. For a full day, the two cut logs and lashed them together, eventually producing a crude but serviceable raft. At sundown of the second day in the canyon, they pushed the raft into the current, jumped on, and began the wildest ride of their lives.

For four days, White and Strole drifted downstream on the current. As they proceeded deeper into the canyon, they noticed the walls rising higher, the shadows cast providing relief from the heat. At sundown, they negotiated the raft toward a gravel bank and made camp. In a short time they exhausted their rations. They grew concerned, for they saw no game at all.

On the morning of the fifth day, the raft entered a stretch of violent rapids. Napping at the stern, White was nearly thrown from the raft, but was grabbed by his hair at the last minute by Strole. For hours, they fought the rapids. By the time they reached calmer water, the two men were exhausted. At the end of the day, they managed to pull onto a narrow strip of sandy shore. After beaching the raft, they fell asleep immediately.

The next morning, after setting out, they encountered more rapids within the first few minutes. These proved to be far worse that those of the previous day, with waves ten to twelve feet high. Terrified, White lashed himself to the raft. Strole decided not to do so and paid for his error in judgment. As White watched, his friend was swept from the raft and drowned.

For hours White rode the violent river, thinking all the while that he was going to die. Around midafternoon, the river became calmer. White was grateful for the slow drifting. Presently, he arrived at a small camp of Hualapai Indians. On spotting them, he called out, and several of the men waded into the slow-moving water and pulled the raft to shore.

Using sign language, White explained that he was hungry, but the Indians refused to provide food. Finally, an old woman passed him a small piece of moldy bread. After eating this, he climbed aboard his raft and continued downstream.

For two more days, White drifted with the current. More rapids were encountered, but none as bad as those that had taken Strole. White lay on the raft, ravenously hungry, barely able to move. Near the end of the second day, White spotted another small camp of Indians along the shore. He took them to be Utes, and they appeared peaceful. He asked for food, but they wanted to know what he had to trade. He offered his revolver, and in return was given the haunch of a small dog. White had no matches and was forced to beg to use the Indians' campfire. He ate the meat half raw, then fell asleep on the raft. The next morning, he proceeded downstream once again.

By nightfall, White decided to beach the raft, get a good night's sleep, and attempt to scale the canyon wall to safety the next morning. He had decided this was the only way out of what seemed to him to be an interminable river. At dawn, he walked along the stream bank until he found a likely spot to attempt his climb. To his surprise, he noticed a series of narrow steps carved into the wall. He observed the erratic zigzag climb up the wall from one ledge to the next. He assumed that if the ancient Indians who once lived in this place had used the steps to come and go, then he could too. Whispering a short prayer, White began his ascent.

By noon, White estimated he was halfway up the wall. It was slow going, and his hunger and exhaustion caused him to stop often. Finally, too tired to continue, he stopped at a ledge that housed a small cave. After making certain no rattlesnakes were about, he crawled into the cave and went to sleep.

The next morning he renewed his effort to climb out of the canyon. After negotiating several vertical yards of difficult climbing, he found himself on another ledge—this one larger than the previous, and with a larger cave. The cave appeared to be deep, and White entered it in hopes of finding something edible. At the far end of the cave, he came upon three large sacks. They appeared to have been fashioned out of Indian blankets and tied at the top with buckskin thongs. Thinking the sacks might contain corn, White attempted to lift one, only to find it was too heavy. Using his pocketknife, he cut the thongs and tipped the bag over. To his astonishment, he found that it was filled with gold nuggets. He opened the second bag and found it likewise contained gold. The third bag held turquoise and several other semiprecious stones he could not identify.

White sat in the cave with the gold for hours, trying to determine whether or not he had gone crazy, wondering if his mind was playing tricks on him. Over and over he ran his hands through the pile of nuggets. They ranged in size, he later said, from a pea to a thumb digit. White estimated there was enough gold in the cave to make him a millionaire. Reality intruded, however, as he began to contemplate the logistics of removing the gold from the cave and transporting it to civilization.

White finally came around to realizing that his primary concern was survival. The gold would do him no good if he was not alive to spend it. He had to get out of the canyon, rest up from his ordeal, and organize a return expedition to retrieve his fortune. That night, he slept in the cave next to the pile of gold nuggets.

The following morning, he selected a large gold nugget and placed it in his pocket. He returned to the ledge and contemplated the rest of his climb. To his dismay, he discovered that while the top of the canyon was only four hundred feet above him, there were no more steps carved into the rock. Further ascent was impossible.

As White contemplated his next move, he realized that the gold must have been lowered to the cave from above. The sacks were far too heavy to have been carried up the steps the way he came. He pondered this until thirst overcame him. He saw the river flowing far below and realized he needed to make his descent before he was too weak to do so.

White spent that night on the raft. In the morning, he found a handful of mesquite beans among a pile of driftwood. He filled his pockets with these, climbed aboard the raft, and shoved out into the current. Eight days later, unconscious and raving, White was found by the Mormon settlers of the tiny community of Callville, Nevada, one hundred miles below the Grand Canyon. For the next several weeks, the Mormons nursed him back to health. Based on the story told to them by White, they estimated he had traveled 550 miles down the river by raft.

White remained in Callville for several months while recuperating. He told his story to the Mormons, and they said, based on his description of the sacks made from blankets and containing the gold and the semiprecious stones, that they must have been made by Zunis.

As time went by, White learned that in 1539, the Zunis were visited by Spanish explorers. The seven pueblo-style villages of these Indians are thought to have given rise to the legend of the Seven Cities of Cíbola, all allegedly rich with gold and other wealth. Oral history of the tribe recalls that the Spaniards were accompanied by a white missionary and a giant black man. The priest, Father Marcos de Niza, announced his mission to convert all of the Indians to Christianity. The black man, Esteban de Dorantes, had other goals. According to one version of the legend, he dressed in skins and gaudy feathers and spent most of his time among the Zunis intimidating the men and assaulting the women. Tired of the bullying by de Dorantes, the Zunis lay in wait for him one afternoon and ambushed him, filling his body with arrows and spears. Following this, they dined on his flesh.

Fearful that the Spanish army would punish them for their deed, the Zunis accumulated their gold and precious stones and carried their wealth to a hiding place in the Grand Canyon. The Zunis knew of a cave that had some sacred meaning to them. They traveled to the location and, using ropes, lowered their wealth from above and placed it into the cave. No one ever knew the location of the hidden Zuni gold until White stumbled upon it by accident in 1867.

White wanted desperately to return to the canyon and retrieve the gold, but he had no idea of the location. He could not recall at which point along the river he had decided to try to climb out, and he doubted he would be able to recognize the location from above.

As the years rolled by, others heard of White's adventure and made attempts to find the Zuni gold. In 1867 and 1868, a number of prospectors and treasure hunters entered the canyon, but all failed in their search. A few lost their lives.

Some time later, two professional treasure hunters arrived in the region to try their luck. Thomas Barnett and Warren Rainsboro listed San Francisco, California, as their hometown. They boasted that they had a long record of success at recovering lost treasures.

Barnett and Rainsboro reasoned that due to the great weight of the gold, the Zunis would pick a canyon-rim location as close to their village as possible. Setting out on horseback from the Zuni village and loaded down with ropes and provisions, the two men traveled for several days, finally arriving at a point on the rim of the canyon. Below, the river made a wide bend toward the north, similar to a description earlier provided by White.

After setting up camp, the two men spent several days exploring along the rim of the canyon. They took turns descending the wall in search of the treasure cave. One man would tie an end of the rope around his waist and the other to the saddle on a mule. He would then lower himself to four hundred feet while the other led the mule along the rim.

For several days their search proved fruitless. They found several caves, a number of skeletons, and a great deal of pottery. On the eighth day, they found the skeletons of two Spanish soldiers, complete with armor and weapons. During the late afternoon of the ninth day, Barnett landed at a narrow ledge that jutted out from a cave. A short distance from where he stood, he could see old, weathered steps that had been cut into the rock. On a hunch, he entered the cave. Inside, he found a large pile of gold nuggets and turquoise. Running outside, he signaled to Rainsboro that he had found the treasure cave. Since it was late in the day, the two men decided to wait until the next day to retrieve the gold.

The following morning, Barnett dropped over the side as Rainsboro backed the mule out providing more rope. Suddenly, the desert quiet was pierced by Barnett's scream. The rope went limp. Leaving the mule, Rainsboro dashed to the edge of the cliff, but could see no sign of his partner. Hauling up the rope, he saw it had been severed, presumably by a sharp rock. Saddened and despondent at the loss of his friend, Rainsboro returned to California. He never again attempted to retrieve the Zuni gold. He refused to discuss the matter with anyone, and his knowledge of the location of the gold was never shared.

When Jim White read the account of Barnett's death, he felt sadness but also vindication. He still possessed the nugget he had carried out in 1867. White never made an attempt to relocate the gold. His desire for riches was tempered by his memories of nearly dying during his journey down the river. All his life he assured people that the Zuni gold was there, hidden away in that remote cave. Someday, he said, someone would find it.

A century and a half after being found by Jim White, the gold is still there.

Geronimo's Gold

The Apache Indians who resided in Arizona traditionally had little use for gold other than for fashioning ornaments. When the early Spanish explorers arrived in the area, they observed the Indians wearing armbands and necklaces made from almost pure gold. Convinced the church would want to know the location of this valuable mineral, the Jesuits befriended the Indians, presenting them with gifts in exchange for information on the whereabouts of their mines.

The priests were taken to a small canyon that opened onto the Verde River. There, they were shown an outcrop of gold from which the Indians procured what they needed. At once, the Spaniards enslaved several of the Indians, chained them together, and forced them to excavate the mineral from the rock matrix. Over the next several weeks, the mine deepened and widened. The vein, the priests discovered, grew thicker and richer.

When the church officials realized that this would be a very profitable mine, the Spaniards decided to construct permanent dwellings in the canyon to house the overseers and the workers. A rock dam was also built to create a reservoir on the small creek that flowed along the bottom of the canyon.

Over the next year and a half, the Spaniards were often attacked by small bands of Apaches who were attempting to free those who were forced to work in the mine. The Europeans slept little, as they were constantly on the alert for the hostile Indians. Sometimes while the Spaniards were sleeping in the dwellings, the Apaches would roll large boulders down onto them from the high canyon walls. Not a week passed when there was not an episode. Unfortunately for the Spaniards, the encounters usually resulted in death.

The Jesuits considered abandoning the mine because of the Indian threat, but it was so rich they were reluctant to leave. Their greed was to haunt them. After eighteen months, the total number of surviving Spaniards was only six, and they began to believe they would not live through another attack.

With survival in mind, the leader of the Spaniards decided it was time to load what gold they had accumulated onto twelve pack mules and leave the canyon for Mexico. Once there, he explained, they would organize a larger and better-armed party and return to the location, subdue the warring Apaches, and resume mining the gold.

As the Spaniards rode out of the canyon the following morning, they were attacked by Indians as they approached the narrow entrance. During the brief fight that followed, several Apaches and four Spaniards were killed. The two survivors managed to turn the mule train around and herd it back to the mine. Once there, the gold ingots were unloaded and stacked just inside the entrance. From this defensive position, the Indians were kept at bay. That night, the two slipped undetected through the Apache lines. With great caution, they traveled southward at night and rested by day. Eventually they reached the mission at Tubac.

As the two surviving Spaniards made plans to return to the canyon and the rich gold mine, King Charles III issued an order from his throne in Europe that all Jesuits were to be expelled from Spain, as well as all of its possessions. As a result, the survivors of the Apache raid abandoned their plans and returned to Mexico City.

After the Spaniards left, the Apaches destroyed all of the rock dwellings. From that point on, they largely avoided the canyon except on those occasions when they needed gold for personal use.

Several years later, noted Apache leader Geronimo learned of the mine and the huge stack of gold ingots just inside the entrance. Aware of the white man's greed for gold, accompanied by the Indian leader's need for rifles and ammunition, the crafty Geronimo would travel to the canyon, remove several of the ingots, and trade them for firearms. It has been estimated that Geronimo, unaware of the true value of the gold, bartered away tens of thousands of dollars worth in order to arm only a few dozen of his followers. In time, the source of the gold became known as Geronimo's Mine.

W. C. Jameson

Regarding the mine, Geronimo swore his warriors to secrecy and told them that anyone who revealed the location would be punished by death. Today, it is said that a few elderly Apaches are still alive who allegedly know the location of this mine, but refuse to tell for fear of reprisal. They claim there are hundreds of gold bars still stacked just beyond the entrance to the shaft. They also claim that no white man will ever find the mine.

Geronimo was eventually captured by the U.S. Army in 1886. In time, he was sent to prison at Fort Sill, Oklahoma. At one point, the Indian tried to convince his captors that in exchange for his freedom, he would tell them the location of a rich gold mine in a remote canyon somewhere in Arizona between Jerome and Perkinsville.

As the officers pondered the offer, Geronimo made clandestine plans to escape. Before he could activate his scheme, however, his duplicity was discovered and he was placed in chains. Geronimo never repeated his offer to reveal the location of the mine, and the secret died with him.

As the years passed, references to the now legendary lost gold mine were encountered in church archives in Mexico City. According to the documents, the mine is located in one of the many small side canyons that enter the Verde River valley. A map describes a rock formation shaped somewhat like the head of an Indian with an exaggerated nose. According to a map that accompanies the description, the mine is located just beneath the nose.

Sometime during the 1930s, a rancher herding some stray cattle out of a remote canyon near the Sycamore River encountered the odd Indian-head-shaped landform. Nearby, he found the remains of two tumbled-down rock structures, along with evidence of what he believed was a rock furnace. Several years later, the rancher learned the story of Geronimo's lost gold mine. Believing he could find it, he decided to return to the location. When he arrived, however, he claimed a rockslide had apparently covered up the opening to the mine.

In 1945, a deer hunter looked down into a small, narrow canyon from a high rim. At the bottom, he said, he could see the remains of two rock dwellings as well as the entrance to what he believed was a mine shaft. He tried to find a way down into the canyon from his position but was unable to do so. As he made his way out of the range, he became lost, making it back to civilization days later. When he attempted to relocate the curious canyon, he could never find it.

Eventually, the story of Geronimo's gold mine faded from the memories of area residents—all of them, that is, save for a handful of older Apaches. The Indians claim that it would be simple to travel to the location and retrieve the gold, but for any of them to provide directions to one outside the tribe would result in death. They believe strongly in this century-old edict, and as a result, remain silent.

The Lost
Oatman Treasure

Not far outside the city limits of Oatman, Arizona, lies a buried treasure in twenty-dollar gold pieces. Lost in 1887, the treasure is estimated to be worth at least one-third of a million dollars today.

In 1857, the Mojave Indians were placed on an Indian reservation adjacent to the Colorado River in present-day Mohave County. The area outside the reservation was soon opened up to settlers, and over the years many of them raised cattle to provide meat for the Indians via government contracts.

One settler, Hiram Smith, saw that a good living could be made selling beef to the government, so he made a bid for the concession. In 1887, he was awarded a contract. On the appointed date, Smith delivered a herd of cattle to Fort Mojave. He hired two herders to drive the animals while he drove a wagon pulled by two horses. Smith was paid $16,000 in twenty-dollar gold coins. After paying off his herders and sending them away, he placed the money into a specially made leather money belt, which he strapped around his waist.

Despite the great weight of the money and the pressing need to return to his ranch, Smith, known to be a hard drinker, made his way to a local saloon to celebrate the cattle sale. Before leaving his ranch, Smith had told his family to come and look for him if he did not make it home by the appointed time. Following several whiskeys, he staggered outside, climbed into his wagon, and headed home.

Smith never made it back to his ranch. One of his family members, along with several neighbors, went to look for him. They concentrated their search along the road between Fort Mojave and a place called

Cottonwood Cove. When they did not find any evidence of his passing, they looked farther to the south. Three days later, the search party came across the abandoned wagon and two dead horses. Instead of turning north toward his ranch after leaving the fort, Smith had turned south. Following his tracks, they found him three miles away near a location called Boundary Cone and not far from the town of Oatman. He was dehydrated and near death. Smith was transported to his ranch, where family members nursed him and prayed for his recovery. Three days after his return, he was lucid enough to explain what had happened.

He had gotten drunk, he told them, and made a wrong turn on the way home. One of the horses pulling the wagon went lame, so Smith pulled to the side of the road and decided to walk the rest of the way. After covering about a mile, the money belt containing the gold coins proved to be too heavy, so he decided to remove it and hide it, intending to return for it at some later date. He dug a shallow hole and placed the money belt within. Casting about for something to mark the cache, he noted that he was in the area of an old abandoned ranch. Nearby he found a clay pot and two rusted horseshoes. He set the pot over the cache and laid the horseshoes inside. He stumbled on for two more miles before passing out.

Smith and his family made plans to return to the site and recover the gold coins as soon as he regained his health. It was not to be. Two weeks after returning home to his ranch, Hiram Smith died of complications from his ordeal.

Two of Smith's sons went in search of the money. Returning to the place where the wagon and horses had been abandoned, they rode across the desert to the location where their father had been found. Rather than following a straight-line route, however, Smith's wanderings had been erratic. Despite several attempts, the sons were never able to locate the gold.

In time, the story of Hiram Smith's lost fortune circulated throughout the area, and hopeful treasure hunters arrived to try to find it. None were successful, and gradually the excitement died down. Years passed, and Hiram Smith and his lost gold-filled money belt were forgotten.

In 1910, rancher P. W. Sayles was riding along his fence line not far from the Colorado River. Now and then, he would stop and repair a broken strand or reset a leaning post. As he replaced his tools in a saddlebag following one repair, Sayles noticed something out of the ordinary

W. C. JAMESON

on the desert floor not far away. Walking over, he saw an old *olla*, the Spanish term for a clay pot. Artifacts, both Indian ones and those from early Spanish and Mexican settlements in the area, were not uncommon. This particular pot, however, was in good condition, so Sayles decided to take it back to the ranch for his wife. When he picked up the olla, he was surprised to find two old horseshoes inside.

Weeks later, the Sayles family had a visitor from a nearby ranch. As the man was leaving, Sayles pointed to the olla and related the circumstances relative to its discovery. The visitor, familiar with the tale of Hiram Smith's lost gold, told him the story, explaining that the contents of the buried money belt contained a fortune in twenty-dollar gold pieces.

Enthused about finding the belt and its contents, Sayles returned to the location where he thought he had found the pot. Since that time, a brief rain shower, as well as high winds, had removed all traces of his presence. Sayles, carrying a shovel, walked miles throughout the desert not far from his fence line in hopes of spotting the place where he found the pot. Now and then, when he was certain he had found it, he would excavate a hole, sometimes several. But he had no luck. Sayles confessed to a friend that he guessed he had dug no less than two hundred holes out in the desert near his fence.

Some time later, Sayles told his story to a man named Fred Bullard, the editor of the Searchlight, Nevada, newspaper. Bullard printed the story, and before long the desert was swarming with hopeful treasure hunters. The money belt and its contents, however, were never found.

Given the current price of gold, along with the antique value of the coins, it has been estimated that, if found today, Hiram Smith's cache would be worth a fortune. Assuming it lies only a few inches from the surface, it is possible that it could be located using a metal detector. The only detail to be worked out is determining where one would need to search along the old fence line.

Wagon Road
Gold Cache

During the late 1800s, a stagecoach road linking Mohave County's Yucca, Arizona, with Needles, California, saw heavy traffic. Coaches and wagons bearing men and equipment working in the area mines regularly plied the route. Today, this northeast/southwest-oriented route is known as the National Old Trails Highway. Somewhere along the old road outside the small town of Yucca lies a buried strongbox containing one million dollars worth of gold ingots, nuggets, and dust.

During the late 1880s, a group of five men rode into the small mining camp of Mineral Park, not far from the town of Chloride in Mohave County. After spending three days drinking in the saloon, they decided to rob it. Making off with $300 in coins and gold dust, the bandits fled south, eventually arriving three days later in Yucca, forty miles away. Unknown to them, a posse consisting of seven men was in pursuit and closing in.

While watering their horses at the Yucca stagecoach station, the bandits heard an intriguing story from one of the employees. A train carrying a strongbox filled with gold bound for a mining company in California was delayed in Kingman because the railroad tracks between that town and Needles had been washed out by flash floods from a recent storm. The locked metal box was placed on a stagecoach for delivery to Needles, where in turn it would be loaded onto another train. The talkative employee told the bandits that the stagecoach carrying the gold was expected in Yucca at any moment.

The five men decided to wait around. A half hour later the coach pulled up. They watched as passengers disembarked, stretched their legs, and entered the station for a meal. Fresh horses were hitched up, and an hour later the stagecoach was on its way toward Needles down the wagon road, a route that would take it through the town of Topock and then across the Colorado River.

A few miles outside Yucca, the bandits caught up with the stagecoach. They shot the driver and guard through the heart and head, respectively, and ordered the passengers out of the coach. After taking money, watches, and other valuables and stowing them in their pockets, they killed them.

After removing the strongbox from the stagecoach, they fired their guns, causing the team of horses to bolt. As the coach disappeared down the road, the bandits broke the lock on the box and opened it. Inside they found gold ingots, nuggets, and dust. They were rich, they determined, but with this revelation came bad news. The box and its contents were far too heavy to transport without a wagon. The bandits decided to return to Yucca, procure a wagon, and return for their wealth. For the time being, they decided, they would hide the box. They alternately pulled and shoved it from the road and several yards into the desert. In the middle of a clump of low-growing brush, they buried it and covered it with debris.

Two hours later, they rode back into Yucca. At the same time they arrived, the posse that was pursuing them from the north showed up and confronted the bandits. A brief gunfight ensued, with two of the lawmen and four of the five bandits getting killed. The surviving bandit was mortally wounded, and as he lay dying on the street, he taunted the lawmen with the information about the stage robbery and the killing of the passengers. The bandit included only cryptic comments about burying the strongbox full of gold.

From the pockets of the bandits, the posse recovered the valuables taken from the slain passengers. The next day, the stagecoach was found just outside the town of Topock, where the horses had finally given out. For days, the posse, accompanied by men from the town of Yucca, searched along the road for any sign of where the strongbox might have been buried, but found none.

From all accounts, the strongbox filled with gold is still there, right where the bandits buried it in the 1880s. Because of the hurried nature of the caching, it is safe to presume the box is only a few inches below the surface.

Lost Stagecoach Loot

During the 1870s, northwestern Arizona was laced with stagecoach routes linking military posts and mining headquarters with the larger cities. Along these routes moved mail, supplies, passengers, and military and mining payrolls. One such route ran from Prescott to Fort Mojave near the Colorado River by way of Kingman. In September 1872, the Fort Mojave–bound coach was transporting mail, passengers, and $72,000 in gold and silver. It was to be used as part of the payroll for the troopers stationed at the fort.

Word of the gold and silver circulated around Kingman well before the stage arrived. Two cowhands, out of work and nearly broke, wondered aloud about the possibilities of robbing the coach. Deciding it would likely be guarded by a cavalry patrol, they set the idea aside. When the coach arrived in town, however, it was not accompanied by a guard contingent. On realizing this, the two men renewed their plans to hold up the coach. They saddled their mounts and rode ahead on the route that snaked its way from Kingman to Fort Mojave through mountain and desert. The two selected a location just past the stage stop at Canyon Station, some twelve miles out of Kingman, and waited in the rocks.

After picking up the mail and resting the team of six horses, the coach driver bid farewell to the station keeper and proceeded on his way. Several hundred yards down the road, two masked gunmen stepped into the path of the coach and commanded the driver to stop. In a short time, they were in possession of a strongbox filled with gold and silver coins. They waved the driver on, but instead of proceeding to Fort Mojave, he turned the stage and headed back to Canyon Station. As he drove away, the driver noted that the two bandits had a difficult time dragging the heavy chest from the road and into the brush.

Back at the station, the driver reported the robbery to the sheriff at Kingman. Within minutes, a posse was assembled and in pursuit of the bandits. When the sheriff and his men arrived at the site of the robbery, they searched the ground for the tracks of the bandits. As they looked for signs, one of the possemen called the sheriff's attention to a column of smoke rising above the trees a hundred yards away. Believing it to be from a campfire made by the stagecoach robbers, the posse proceeded with caution.

The two bandits, oblivious to the potential for pursuit and having decided to prepare dinner, were surprised to see the lawmen riding toward them. A brief gunfight ensued and one of the robbers was killed. The second mounted his horse and attempted to flee, but was captured within minutes. After arresting the man, the sheriff queried him about the location of the stolen strongbox. The bandit refused to answer. The sheriff and posse members searched the area from the road to the bandits' campsite, but found neither strongbox nor evidence of where it might have been buried.

The bandit was taken to Kingman, where he was eventually tried and sentenced to a long term in the Yuma Territorial Prison. Several searches near Canyon Station for the strongbox containing the gold and silver were conducted by law enforcement as well as stagecoach officials—all for naught.

In 1935, sixty-three years after the stagecoach robbery, an old man arrived at the location of what was left of Canyon Station and set up a crude camp nearby. From time to time the elderly man was seen walking along the old stagecoach road as if he were searching for something.

The owner of the land where the old man was camped was a rancher named Goodwill. Goodwill had seen the old fellow now and then as he was out working his cattle, but never found the time to approach him. Since the visitor appeared harmless, Goodwill felt no hurry about it. Then one day as he was finishing some chores, the rancher was riding along the old road when he spotted the elderly man poking around the ruins of the old stagecoach station. Goodwill reined up, dismounted, and went over to introduce himself.

During the course of the ensuing conversation, Goodwill learned that the old man had recently been released from prison. Then, he related an amazing story. He said his cell mate for more than twenty years at the Yuma prison had been serving time for robbing the Prescott–Fort Mojave stagecoach back in 1872. The cell mate had told him that after hiding a strongbox filled with gold and silver coins, he and his partner were found by a sheriff's posse. The friend was killed, and the surviving robber was sent to prison for a long stretch.

After they had been cell mates for twenty years, the two prisoners had become close friends. One day, the stagecoach robber learned that he was dying and did not have long to live. Before he died, he told his friend he wanted to leave directions relative to where the strongbox was hidden so that he could retrieve it when he got out of the penitentiary. As the dying man spoke of distances and landmarks, the friend wrote them down.

Goodwill told the old man it was fine to hunt for the lost treasure on his property. He even negotiated a percentage cut should anything be located. The old man agreed, and for the next several days was seen pursuing his search throughout the immediate area. One afternoon, the old man approached Goodwill as he was working near his barn. He told the rancher that he would be packing up and heading on, and that the search for the lost strongbox had proven fruitless. He explained that many of the landmarks mentioned by his late cell mate no longer existed, and that it was impossible to tell where the gold and silver coins had been cached. Goodwill said there had been at least two major fires in the area since he had owned the property, and both had burned off a significant portion of the forest near where the old man searched. He also told the old man that the road he was seen walking along was not the original stagecoach road. The new one had been made by the previous rancher, and it was difficult to determine the exact location of the original. Fire and floods had dramatically changed the characteristics of the landscape during the previous six decades.

Discouraged, the old man bade Goodwill goodbye and left, never to return. For the next few years, rancher Goodwill searched for the strongbox himself, but had no more luck than the old man. Obligations related to operating his ranch prevented him from investing a great amount of time into looking for the treasure.

The strongbox filled with gold and silver coins taken during the 1872 robbery has never been found and still lies hidden somewhere not far off the old stagecoach road leading from Canyon Station to Fort Mojave.

Northeast

De Espejo's Lost
Canyon of Gold

During the last half of the sixteenth century, great extents of the North American continent west of the Mississippi River were being systematically explored by mounted and armed parties of Spaniards accompanied by church officials and mining engineers. In addition to examining potential sites for settlement and agriculture, the objectives of such journeys also included the prospecting for and mining of precious metals, in particular gold and silver. Once ore was discovered, mining operations commenced and processing facilities were established. The ore was formed into ingots, and several times each year the accumulated gold or silver was transported to governmental headquarters in Mexico City and thence to the treasury in Spain.

One such company of soldiers, monks, and miners was commanded by Antonio de Espejo. In 1583, de Espejo led his contingent into a maze of canyons located in the southern part of what is today Coconino County and not far from the town of Sedona. Concerned that he was lost, de Espejo ordered his men to establish camp while he sent out scouts to find a trail that would take them to the open country they thought lay some distance to the north. As preparations for a meal were under way that evening, two of the mining engineers discovered a thick vein of gold along the wall of a nearby narrow canyon. They hastened to notify de Espejo.

Impressed with the quality of the ore, de Espejo decided to remain at that location and undertake the mining of the gold. During the next several weeks, soldiers were put to work constructing living quarters out of timber and rock, both of which were plentiful in the verdant canyon. As this was going on, de Espejo sent two platoons of soldiers to the south in search of Indians. The soldiers were to capture as many as they were able and return them to the canyon, where they would be chained together at the neck and put to work in the mines.

One week later, the soldiers returned with one hundred Indian captives. After being manacled and chained, they were forced to dig the gold ore from several locations in the narrow canyon. For three months the gold was mined and processed into ingots, which were in turn stacked inside one of the shafts awaiting transportation to Mexico City.

De Espejo grew comfortable with his mining enterprise, until one day the canyon was filled with hostile Indians who expressed their objection to the enslavement of their kin. The commander decided to ignore the protestors, concluding that he possessed the men and arms to repel them if necessary. Each day, however, Spanish hunting parties were attacked and killed. Several nighttime raids on the encampment resulted in the deaths of more than a dozen soldiers.

After losing a number of men and finding the replenishment of fresh meat in jeopardy as a result of the increasing guerilla warfare, de Espejo grew frustrated. He decided it would be best to abandon the canyon for the time being. After loading up the accumulated ingots onto burros, he had several maps made of the location. This done, he led his command from the area and returned to Mexico.

De Espejo never returned to the canyon. With the passage of time, his maps, along with his personal diary describing the location of the mines, were placed in the archives of a Catholic church in Mexico City. Twenty years later, the documents were found by newly assigned church officials. Excited by the prospect of riches, they organized an expedition to travel to the remote canyon and reopen the mines. According to church records, this was done and an impressive amount of gold was harvested over the next several years.

During the beginning of the seventeenth century, increasing difficulties with the Spanish government as well as with the church began interfering with various mining activities throughout the American West. The war in Europe demanded the increasing attention of Spanish officials. To ensure enough manpower, soldiers were withdrawn from the New World and shipped back to Spain. Growing dissension within the ranks of the Catholic church also proved distracting and debilitating. To compound these problems, a general uprising of Indians and increasing hostility toward the Spanish invaders led to more warfare. All of these difficulties combined to force the abandonment of hundreds of the mines operated by the government and the church. In time, miners and priests withdrew from the narrow canyon discovered by de Espejo. Before returning to Mexico, they closed the mines, covering the openings with rocks and brush to make them appear as a normal part of the environment.

In 1719, yet another group of priests discovered de Espejo's diary and maps in the church archives. Like those before them, these holy men organized yet another major expedition to the remote canyon. Accompanying them was a company of soldiers and a contingent of mining engineers. As the party traveled through northern Mexico, they captured and enslaved two hundred Opata Indians, chained them together, and marched them the remaining 250 miles to the mines, where they were put to work. The priests told the Indians they were doing God's work. The Indians, who often worked eighteen hours a day, slept in the open and were provided with poor rations. Many died from exposure, hunger, and overwork. The priests and soldiers repaired and moved into the living quarters that remained from the previous expeditions.

What turned out to be a highly successful mining operation continued until around 1760. During the course of nearly two centuries, the mines were operated by the Spaniards, and hundreds of burro loads of gold ingots were transported from Arizona to church headquarters in Mexico City, thus enriching the Catholic treasury beyond the wildest dreams of the papist administrators. Then, within a few short weeks, the canyon was suddenly abandoned and no explanation was ever provided by the church. The Spaniards left in a hurry and never returned. Some researchers have concluded that another Indian uprising forced the abandonment of the canyon, but that is based on speculation.

From all indications, the canyon of gold remained unoccupied, even forgotten, for almost one hundred years. Then, in 1853, a lone horseman, fleeing a group of Hualapai Indians who had attacked and killed his three companions while they were prospecting several miles to the south, chanced upon the location. As he rode into the narrow gorge, the horseman, Clifford Haines, encountered several log and rock structures, as well as evidence of extensive mining in the past. Following an initial inspection of the area, Haines realized that the site had been abandoned for many years, but had once apparently accommodated a population of over two hundred people. From where he stood among the crude dwellings, Haines could see the openings to several mines in the nearby canyon wall. While inspecting three of the shafts, he retrieved a dozen large pieces of rich gold ore and found several seams of gold that appeared promising. Determined to put together a party of miners and return to the canyon, Haines placed the gold in his saddlebags and, wary of pursuing Indians, fled the area.

After reaching Tucson days later, Haines organized a group of men to accompany him back to the canyon. He made plans to leave within a few days after procuring supplies, but was killed the following morning when a horse fell on him.

In 1874, a man named John T. Squires arrived in Santa Fe with a very old and tattered map that purportedly showed the location of several gold mines in a remote location in Coconino County. After recruiting a small party of miners, he traveled to the area and, according to reports, located de Espejo's lost canyon of gold. After cleaning out and moving into the old dwellings, Squires and his men reopened two of the most promising shafts.

After replacing the rotten timber supports, the Squires party extracted and processed a quantity of gold. Seeing the potential of the mines, Squires and his workers returned to Santa Fe to purchase more supplies and mining equipment. While in town, Squires decided to hire more men to dig the ore. After returning to the canyon a few weeks later, he was dismayed to find it occupied by dozens of Indians.

The miners set up camp near the mouth of the canyon, not daring to venture farther for fear of the Indians. A short time after arriving, Squires and two of the men rode away in search of wild game for the cooking pots. While they were several miles away, the Indians attacked. All of the miners were killed and their tents set afire.

Hours later, as Squires and his companions were riding back toward the canyon, they spotted smoke rising above the trees. Fearing the worst, Squires ordered his friends to remain while he rode ahead. As Squires entered the canyon, he looked upon the death and destruction wrought by the Indians. He dismounted and, after tying his horse to a bush, crept forward, keeping cover behind rocks and trees.

A few hundred yards beyond the camp, he saw several of the Indians sealing the mine entrances with rocks and debris. Within seconds he was spotted and a half-dozen warriors gave chase. Squires raced back to his horse, mounted up, and rode back to his two companions. Together, the three fled the range.

Squires traveled to New Mexico determined to organize a larger, well-armed party, one better prepared to deal with the Indians and reopen the mines. As he was making plans for a return trip, however, he was killed in a gunfight in Taos. The only item found in his possession was a map showing the location of the canyon, but it was accidentally burned a few days later.

In 1889, following the end of the Indian threat in Arizona, several members of Squires's original party attempted to return to the canyon, but were never able to relocate it.

In 1896, a man named William Howard accidentally found the lost canyon of gold. Hired to provide meat for the workers laying the track for the Santa Fe Railroad, Howard rode into the canyon one afternoon in search of game. He found several old tumbled-down and burned dwellings and located numerous articles that had once belonged to members of the Squires mining party. When several months later Howard related his experience to two veteran prospectors, they told him he had likely encountered the famous gold discoveries of de Espejo and John T. Squires. Convinced he had surely found the lost canyon of gold, Howard, along with several friends, attempted to travel to it and reopen the mines. On reentering the region, however, Howard became confused and lost and unable to recognize pertinent landmarks. Ultimately, he failed to find the right canyon.

Howard refused to give up, however, and continued to search for the lost mines over the next eight years. One day he rode into Flagstaff and announced that he had finally located them. He described the narrow canyon, the old stone and timber structures, and the covered-over mine entrances. Howard confided to several acquaintances that he was in the process of removing some of the rock debris from one of the mine openings and expected to have it cleared within a few weeks. He continued to return to the mines for several days at a time for nearly a year, but ceased providing information to friends. Howard passed away in 1916, and if he ever removed any gold from the canyon, he never told anyone.

In the 1920s, a cowhand entered the canyon searching for stray cattle. Four days later, he rode into ranch headquarters and reported finding some old ruins. He described them as tumbled-down rock and timber structures. He also claimed to have seen a number of mine shafts that appeared as though someone had tried to conceal them under rockfalls. At the time, the significance of the canyon was unknown to him, and he never returned. Years later, however, he learned of the potential of his discovery from some area old-timers, but by then he was too old and infirm to undertake a search.

During the mid-1930s a pilot, flying low over the region, detected the remains of a number of old dwellings at the bottom of a remote narrow canyon in south Coconino County. He informed some friends who made a hobby of searching for and collecting archeological artifacts. After receiving directions from the pilot, they found the canyon and the ruins and explored the area for a full afternoon. Disappointed at finding nothing of value, and having no interest whatsoever in abandoned mine shafts, they left, never to return.

In 1937, a resident of Virginia who was staying at a guest ranch in Oak Creek Canyon decided to take a long hike through a maze of ridges and valleys he knew existed a short distance away. Carrying a small pack filled with provisions and a camera, he struck out on the trail for an extended journey into the picturesque back country. Two days later, he wandered into a remote canyon and took several photographs of some long-abandoned dwellings he found there. After returning to the guest ranch, he had his pictures developed and showed them to fellow visitors and employees. An old cowboy who was in charge of the riding stock at the ranch saw the photos. Familiar with the story of de Espejo's lost canyon of gold and Squires's subsequent experiences, he realized the importance of the hiker's discovery. He told the visitor the tales of lost gold, and together the two men attempted to return to the site; but the hiker became confused and lost, and they were never able to find it.

In 1946, the son of the Virginia man who stayed at the guest ranch, accompanied by a friend, traveled to the region to try to find the lost canyon of gold. Using his father's photographs as a guide, the two men attempted to retrace the route taken by the father. While they were able to identify many of the landmarks in the photos, they claimed that over the years the character of the region had changed as a result of forest fires and flash floods. After several days of searching, they gave up and returned home.

The search for the lost canyon of gold discovered by Antonio de Espejo continues today. With the passage of time, new forest growth, and the ongoing processes of erosion and weathering, it becomes more difficult to find. Rediscovered several times in the past, it will likely be found again in the future. Eventually, some fortunate hunter of lost mines, or a hiker, will stumble onto the ruins, explore the old mines, and find the fortune in gold ore still lying within the rock matrix of the deep canyon walls.

Lost Monument
Valley Silver Mine

M onument Valley, located in northeastern Arizona and southeastern Utah, is a unique environment dominated by sandstone mesas,
buttes, and spires, all resulting from the mass erosion of the adjacent softer
rock. This picturesque landscape is the homeland of the Navajo and Ute
Indians, and for centuries they ruled this special geography.

For years, early white settlers in this area heard tales of rich silver ore
that could be found in the valley. Prospectors and geologists, however,
denounced the idea, maintaining that the precious metal could not possibly be associated with the sedimentary rock that dominates this region.
In spite of contentions from the experts, however, Navajos were known to
have mined silver in this area for many generations to fashion the bracelets,
rings, necklaces, and other items they used to adorn themselves. The silver,
according to the Indians, was so pure and rich that it needed no refining,
and it could be worked into desired shapes as it came from the ground.

Longtime Colorado prospector James Merrick had heard the stories
of silver being mined by the Indians in Monument Valley and believed
there was some truth behind the tales. Intrigued, he decided to investigate. Teaming up with a young man named Mitchell, Merrick acquired
some supplies, pack animals, and equipment and went in search of the
precious metal in the fall of 1879.

During this time, the Navajo and Ute Indians who inhabited Monument Valley were hostile to white intruders. Many who entered the realm
of the red man were attacked, killed, and mutilated as an example to others who might dare to cross the region.

Carefully avoiding the Indians, Merrick and Mitchell explored the
valley in the area of Skeleton Mesa for several weeks. Their efforts were

rewarded when they finally located the silver mine. At first they were unsure that it was the one they sought. The mesa itself was singularly unimpressive and barely distinguishable from others in the area. Low and narrow, the shaft extended into dangerously weathered rock only a short distance. At the end of the shaft, however, Merrick found a rich seam of almost pure ore. Within a few days, the two men dug out enough of the silver to fill several leather packs.

Merrick and Mitchell returned to Durango, Colorado, where they had the metal assayed. They learned it was nearly pure, possessing only traces of lead and zinc. Enthused by the prospect of great wealth, the two men purchased more supplies and within a few days were on their way back to Monument Valley.

Merrick and Mitchell worked hard, long days in the small mine for almost three months. They followed the vein of ore deeper into the rock. In time, they had accumulated enough silver to load three stout mules. As the two men were beginning to believe they would soon retire to a life of wealth and luxury, their luck took a turn for the worse. The Utes discovered them.

For several days, the two miners noticed Indians observing them from afar. Each day the number of watchers grew. Each day they grew bolder, venturing ever closer to the camp. Concerned that an attack was imminent, Merrick decided to take what silver they had gathered and leave at the first opportunity. The next morning, after breakfast, they loaded the mules with their ore and equipment and rode away from Skeleton Mesa. Behind them came the Utes, closing the distance with each passing mile.

An hour later, the two miners rounded a turn in the trail and were surprised to see twenty Ute horsemen positioned in front of them, blocking their passage. The leader of the Indians, a squat, evil-looking man known as No-Neck, rode up to Merrick and Mitchell. No-Neck had a reputation for despising white men and swore to kill all who entered his domain. As the chief stopped in front of the two men, the remaining warriors circled the trio.

Using sign language, No-Neck demanded tobacco from the miners. Merrick, believing their safety lay in demonstrating courage instead of giving in to Indian demands, refused. He ordered No-Neck and his warriors to disperse and allow them to proceed.

At a signal from the scowling chief, the mounted warriors fired arrows into Merrick and Mitchell. The two men never had a chance.

W. C. Jameson

Mitchell, pierced by more than a dozen wooden shafts, toppled from his horse and was dead before he hit the ground. Merrick, impaled by at least six arrows, somehow managed to spur his horse and broke through the line of Indians. He rode at top speed for three miles until his mount finally gave out and dropped. Several Utes who trailed Merrick found the wounded man crawling across the stony desert pavement forty yards from his dead horse. For the next half hour, the Utes used Merrick for target practice, hurling their lances into him time and again.

No-Neck and his followers took the horses, mules, saddles, equipment, and what few canned goods the miners possessed. They also removed clothing and boots from the dead men. Cutting loose the leather sacks filled with silver, the Indians let them drop to the desert floor next to the body of Mitchell. As the Indians rode away, the desert winds were already shifting the loosely consolidated surface layers of sand, blowing the particles along the ground to accumulate on the windward side of objects lying in the path.

Several months later when a party of soldiers passed through Monument Valley, they discovered the grisly skeletons of Merrick and Mitchell partially buried in the sand. Within only a few feet of Mitchell's body, and under a thin cover of sand, were several leather sacks that contained a small fortune in silver ore. The soldiers never suspected their existence.

The story of Merrick and Mitchell and their rich mine soon spread throughout much of the Southwest, and many were inspired to search for it. Most of those who attempted to enter Monument Valley, however, were killed or driven away by the Indians.

One adventurer who was not deterred by the threat of hostile Utes was a man named Cassidy Hite. Hite not only entered Monument Valley, he spent his days in search of the mysterious Indian silver mine from which Merrick and Mitchell dug the ore. Hite somehow managed to make friends with Navajo Indians who, in turn, afforded some protection from the hostile Utes.

One day Hite was searching for the mine in the company of a Navajo companion. While the two explored the area around Skeleton Mesa, the Indian reined up, dismounted, and picked up a small black rock. He showed it to Hite, who immediately recognized it as silver.

For the next three months, Hite concentrated his searches in the Skeleton Mesa area. One day he was rewarded by the discovery of a leather sack filled with silver nuggets. Hite presumed that Merrick and Mitchell had accidentally dropped the sack while attempting to flee from the Utes years earlier.

Further searching yielded only discouragement, and Hite decided to abandon his attempts to locate the mine. Weeks later, as he was seated at a campfire with an elderly Navajo, Hite listened as the old man related a story about journeying when he was a young boy to a small and little-known Indian silver mine located near Skeleton Mesa. The mine, he told Hite, was the source of much of the silver the Navajos used to make their prized ornaments and jewelry. According to the Indian, the ore was so pure it could be carved from the vein with a pocketknife. When Hite pressed the old man for directions to the mine, the Navajo told him the location was a secret known only to a few of the older Indians. Despite his pleas, the old man refused to tell Hite the location of the mine, explaining that the penalty for such was death.

Several Indians who have lived all their lives in or near Monument Valley were interviewed in 1988 about the tale of the lost silver mine. Except for one elderly Navajo, none ever claimed to have heard of it. The old one, however, admitted that the mine did exist and was known of by only a few. Its actual location, he claimed, had been forgotten. All the old man knew was that the mine was located in Monument Valley near Skeleton Mesa.

W. C. JAMESON

The Lost Silver
Creek Mine

The old prospector knew silver ore when he saw it, and he was convinced that the vein he chanced upon on the slope of a low mountain not far from the east bank of Silver Creek in Navajo County would prove to be a rich deposit. He set a charge of dynamite in order to remove some of the rock matrix and expose more of the vein. Following the blast, the old man examined the opening and congratulated himself on his work. He picked up one of the large chunks of ore that had been blown loose from the rock matrix and realized he had discovered a vein of argentite, an unusual and valuable silver ore that was ruby red. Argentite was purer than other kinds of silver, and the prospector estimated it would assay out to 80 percent or better.

After years of toiling in mines throughout the Southwest, the old man, Mark Carpenter, realized on this warm July day in 1885 that he would soon be rich. For years, he had worked for others in silver mines throughout Colorado and Nevada. Quitting those, he decided to go out on his own, but had few successes, earning just enough to finance his next prospecting trip. From his years of experience, however, Carpenter was well versed in recognizing precious metals, and the ore he held in his hands was the richest he had ever seen.

Days earlier, Carpenter had set out claim markers—cone-shaped stacks of rocks within which was a Prince Albert tobacco can containing a description of his claim. Now, he realized, he needed to travel to St. Johns, forty miles to the east, to register a formal claim.

The following morning, Carpenter rose early, ate a cold breakfast, and packed his two burros with food and gear and several pounds of the rich silver ore. He led his burros up the trail that paralleled Silver Creek.

Farther ahead was a fork in the trail. The eastern fork led to the small town of Shumway a few miles away. The west fork would take him to St. Johns. As he walked and led his burros, Carpenter kept a watchful eye out for Apaches who were known to attack and kill lone travelers in this isolated part of the country.

Carpenter had traveled another couple of miles when he heard two rifle shots. At the same time, he felt a sharp pain in his right shoulder and chest as the slugs ripped through him. He dropped to the ground. Convinced he had been attacked by Indians, he was certain he was going to die.

With unbearable pain and bleeding profusely, Carpenter dragged his rifle behind him and crawled into a thicket. From the brushy cover, he examined the area from which he thought his attackers had fired, but saw and heard nothing. After another two hours, convinced his attackers had departed, Carpenter crawled out of his hiding place and managed to walk over to his burros. With difficulty, he climbed onto one of them and positioned himself across the wooden pack saddle and panniers. Using his rifle, he prodded the animal up the trail, hoping to reach safety. The second burro remained at the site, grazing on a patch of nearby grass. During the ride, Carpenter passed out and dropped his weapon.

Unknown to the miner, Troop A of the Fourth Cavalry stationed at Fort Apache was camped only a mile up the creek. Around midafternoon, one of the army scouts alerted post commander Captain A. A. Smith that a burro was approaching the camp and that it appeared to be transporting a dead man. By the time Smith reached the burro, two scouts had tied it to the low branch of a tree and had laid the rider out on the ground. Smith examined the man and saw that he was badly wounded, perhaps mortally. At that point, Carpenter regained consciousness, provided a brief explanation of what had happened, and begged for water.

By this time, several of the soldiers from the camp had arrived. Smith assigned four of them to carry the man to the infirmary. An hour later, post surgeon John Fisher exited the hospital tent and reported to Captain Smith, explaining that the old man had no chance to live. Smith instructed the doctor to see that the old man was comfortable and well cared for during his final hours.

Fisher sat with Carpenter for the rest of the day and into the night. During that time, the old man told Fisher of his silver discovery at a point near Silver Creek only a few miles away. He described the vein, the

W. C. JAMESON

mine, and provided a landmark or two. He pulled several small nuggets of argentite from his pocket and presented them to the surgeon.

Carpenter told Fisher that he guessed some renegade Apaches shot him and then rode away. He also mentioned that when he recovered, he would return to his mine, remove as much of the argentite as he could carry on his burros, and retire a wealthy man. It was not to be. That night Carpenter died from loss of blood. He was buried in a shallow grave a few yards from the camp.

While Carpenter was being interred, a sergeant came to Captain Smith's tent and advised him that he needed to take a look at the old prospector's belongings. When Smith arrived at the point where the enlisted man had unloaded the panniers, he spotted a small pile of what he recognized as a particular type of silver ore called argentite. After examining it, he concluded that a small fortune in rare silver lay before him. Smith also concluded that the old man was on his way to St. Johns to file a claim for his mine. Intrigued, Smith elected to try to find the mine himself.

On the pretense of back-trailing the prospector down Silver Creek to the site of the ambush to see if Apaches might have been involved, Smith assembled a detail of ten troopers and two scouts and set out. A short time later, they arrived at the scene. On the ground was a spot of blood the size of a dinner plate. The scouts noted that two riders had arrived at the site and led a second burro away down the trail. One of the scouts found the place where two men had sat in hiding prior to ambushing the prospector. Two empty .30-30 rounds lay on the ground among the boot prints. The ambushers were not Indians, but white men.

Smith and the detail followed the tracks, but the two riders had been galloping their mounts, apparently intent on getting as far away from the scene of the crime as possible. On the return trip back to the camp, Smith kept an eye out for any sign of Carpenter's silver mine, but found nothing. Over the next several weeks, Captain Smith made several more attempts to try to find the mine, without success.

On his days off, post surgeon John Fisher also searched for the mine, using the directions he obtained from Carpenter—directions he shared with no one else. On several occasions Fisher believed he was close to the mine, but in each case he was forced to return to camp because of the threat of Apaches, storms, or other reasons.

Weeks later, on returning to Fort Apache, Fisher carried the nuggets the prospector had given him to an assayer and learned they tested out at 84 percent pure. According to the assayer, it was the richest ore yet found in Arizona.

Three years later, at Fort Union, Dr. John Fisher had completed his commitment to the army and was discharged. He began to make plans to return to Silver Creek near Shumway and search for Mark Carpenter's lost argentite mine. He enlisted the help of Anderson Swallow, a recently discharged sergeant. Together, the two men acquired several mules, supplies, and mining equipment. In addition, Fisher purchased the materials necessary to conduct assays on minerals. Within a month, following their separation from the army, the partners were on their way to Silver Creek.

During the three years that had passed since Carpenter's death, several claims had been filed along Silver Creek. In addition, a number of homesteaders had taken up residence in the area. As Fisher and Swallow explored along the creek, they were chased off at gunpoint several times by suspicious and defensive miners.

Using the directions and descriptions provided by Carpenter, Fisher selected a portion of the mountains to explore. Here and there, the two men found traces of argentite in the upper portions of Silver Creek. They deduced that the silver had washed into the creek from some location above, so they concentrated their searches along the slopes.

Weeks passed, and finally they encountered evidence of previous mining at a location about four miles from the old Fourth Cavalry campground. West of the creek was a low, shallow tunnel that had been blasted into the rock. But nowhere in the tunnel could be found a vein of argentite.

A short distance from this mine, Fisher and Swallow came to a conical boundary marker. They tore it down and found a Prince Albert can inside. When they withdrew the piece of paper from within, it was so dried out that it fell apart. Several dozen yards away, they found the remains of another marker. It appeared to have been torn down.

Days passed, and Fisher and Swallow found two more shallow mines. They were short tunnels blasted into the rock, just as Carpenter had described, but only one contained a vein of argentite, and it was only an inch thick. More time passed, and the two men decided to travel to Shumway to rest themselves and their mules while deciding what to do next.

At Shumway, Fisher suggested they return to the tunnel that contained the thin vein of silver. He had a good feeling about it, he said,

W. C. JAMESON

and wanted to check it out again. After resupplying themselves, they returned to Silver Creek and the tunnel Fisher had targeted. They set dynamite charges and opened up another ten feet of the shaft. Much to their delight, the small silver vein had widened to several inches in thickness. Fisher ran an assay on the mineral, and while it never reached 84 percent like Carpenter's ore, it proved rich enough to work.

The next morning as Swallow climbed out of his bedroll and rose to start the fire for breakfast, he was shot down from ambush. Fisher grabbed his rifle and positioned himself behind a tree and scanned the area for the shooter. He thought his partner had been killed, but was relieved when he saw Swallow crawling for cover behind a nearby rock.

From the trees came another rifle shot. Fisher fired off three rounds at the sound and heard a man cry out. Believing the assailant to be sufficiently distracted, Fisher raced to Swallow. He discovered that his partner had suffered a shoulder wound, and it appeared that a bone was broken. He fashioned a bandage from Swallow's shirt and applied it in haste. From his medical kit, he withdrew a painkiller and administered it.

Minutes passed, and several more shots came from the woods, striking near where Fisher and Swallow cowered behind the rock. More time passed, and then a voice called out, warning the two men to pack up their belongings and leave. The voice said the mine belonged to him.

As Fisher loaded gear and supplies onto the mules, he heard sounds of a scuffle in the woods. Presently, a second voice called out, informing him that the bushwhacker who shot at them had been subdued and was being brought down to the camp. Two men who Fisher identified as prospectors he had met on the previous trip pushed a man before them, prodding him with their rifle barrels. Following a short discussion, the five men set out for St. Johns. Fisher wanted to get his partner to a doctor and file a claim on the mine. He also wanted to turn their assailant over to the sheriff.

During the trip, Swallow developed a high fever and was delirious. Fisher learned there was no doctor in town, so he rented a room above a tavern and attempted to nurse his partner back to health. He turned the assailant over to the sheriff, but the man was released after a few days.

Swallow grew worse, and several weeks passed before he was able to get out of bed and walk around. While Swallow was convalescing, Fisher made friends with the owner of the town's mercantile, Solomon Barth. Fisher told Barth about Mark Carpenter's lost mine and the vein of argentite he and Swallow had found near Silver Creek. Barth grew interested and asked to become a partner. Fisher declined, but when Swallow suffered a setback and Fisher ran out of money, he agreed to sell the mine to the merchant. After receiving $10,000 from Barth, Fisher took Swallow by train to Albuquerque, New Mexico, to be treated. It took six months, but he finally recovered.

When Swallow was able to ride, Fisher suggested they return to Silver Creek and make another attempt to locate Carpenter's mine. When they arrived at St. Johns, Barth told them he had hired a crew of three Mexicans to work the claim he had purchased. They encountered even greater thickness of the argentite vein as they tunneled deeper until they eventually came to a large pocket of the ore. After removing that, the vein thinned out and the mine was abandoned. Barth told them that after purchasing supplies and paying off his workers, he had doubled his investment.

Barth's success reinforced the notion that argentite in paying quantities could be found in the area. Fisher and Swallow were convinced that if they could locate the original mine found by Carpenter, they would be able to live the remainder of their lives as wealthy men.

For another year the two men searched for the lost argentite mine, to no avail. Swallow returned to New Mexico and went into cattle ranching. Fisher decided to open up his own medical practice.

When interviewed twenty years later, Fisher stated that he was convinced a rich argentite mine existed somewhere near Silver Creek, that Carpenter's find was yet to be relocated. He recalled the 84 percent pure assay he had conducted, and knew there could be no doubt of Carpenter's veracity. Fisher acknowledged that he and his partner had erred in believing the mine was near the creek. After years of thinking about it, he grew certain that the mine was in the mountains some distance away.

Since Fisher's time, argentite has been found with some regularity along Silver Creek. Carpenter's rich mine, however, has never been relocated.

Coconino County's Lost Gold Ingots

A hidden hoard of gold ingots and coins acquired in a series of robberies has lured treasure hunters into the Mogollon Plateau region of Coconino County in northeastern Arizona for over a century. Several have searched for this lost treasure over the years, and at least one man claimed to have found it. He died before he could return to retrieve it.

Henry Tice, twenty-three years old, was an out-of-work cowhand. Deciding that prospects for a job might be better in California, he tied his few belongings to the back of his saddle and rode out of Tucson one early morning in April 1879. He was joined by two friends: Tom James and Guppy O'Reilly. James, thirty, had made a living robbing isolated miners in California until he was identified and run out of the state. O'Reilly, in his forties, was a prospector who had yet to make a strike. On the second day out, they encountered four more travelers who were likewise down on their luck.

After several days on the trail, the seven men were seated around their campfire when they heard the sound of an approaching stagecoach traveling from the south and heading toward the town of Gila Bend. Having less than one dollar between them, they decided to stop the stage and rob it. They mounted up. As the coach slowed to cross a dry, sandy stream bottom, four of the riders, revolvers drawn, approached the vehicle from the right side while the other three closed in from the left. After stopping the coach, Tice ordered the driver and guard to throw the metal case and a wooden chest to the ground. When this was done, he told them to continue on.

When the coach disappeared down the road, the bandits broke the lock on the case and smashed the chest to bits. Expecting to find just enough money to get them to California, they were stunned to discover $125,000 in gold coins, and twenty-two brick-sized gold ingots. Each of the ingots had the word "AJO" stamped onto it, indicating they had come from the Ajo mining district several miles to the south. They estimated the ingots to be worth $200,000.

After removing the contents, the bandits made room for the gold in their saddlebags. Not wishing to remain in their camp in case a posse came looking for them, they mounted up and continued their westward trek. Around dusk of the following day, Tice and his companions spurred their weary mounts up to the Shawnix Stage Station. When the operator and cook stepped outside to greet the newcomers, Tice pulled a gun on them and tied them up. Inside the station they found more loot: two more iron boxes containing a total of $140,000 in gold coins along with $60,000 in currency. The shipment was awaiting a morning pickup.

The bandits forced the cook to prepare a big dinner for them. When they finished eating, they took three mules from the corral and loaded the station loot onto them. After stealing food, a barrel of blasting powder, and some blasting caps and fuses, they rode away, changing their course from west to north. They rode for days without seeing anyone. Travel was slow because of the overloaded horses and mules. As the temperatures in the low desert soared, the bandits decided to make their way to the cooler elevations they knew existed toward the northeast. In time, they found themselves setting up camp in a timbered section of the Tonto Basin, about fifty miles north of Phoenix.

Two days following the robbery of the Shawnix Station, the owner returned. King Woolsey was a well-known figure in Arizona. Having arrived in 1860, he had gained a reputation as an Indian fighter, lawman, mine owner, and successful cattleman. He owned a large ranch at Agua Caliente east of Yuma, and a farm in the Salt River Valley not far from Phoenix. In a short time, Woolsey assembled a posse of sixteen men, including eleven Pima Indians, and went in search of the bandits.

After resting the men and stock for two days, the bandits rode up Tonto Creek. Tice, James, and O'Reilly rode far in the lead, the other four bringing up the rear. Along the way, Tice and his two friends passed a family of Apaches camped alongside the creek. The riders waved and the Indians returned the greeting. Moments later, as the three rode beyond a

W. C. JAMESON

bend in the stream, they heard the sound of gunfire behind them. They reined up, and a few minutes later the four trailing riders arrived. Grinning, they told of killing all the Apaches in the small camp.

Tice explained to them that they might have made the biggest mistake of their lives. As soon as other members of the tribe learned of the massacre, he said, they would not rest until the killers were hunted down and slain. Tice suggested that the best thing to do was to ride as fast as possible toward Mogollon Rim, which lay forty miles to the northeast. Once into the thick-timbered canyon area, they stood a better chance of defending themselves and perhaps escaping from any pursuing Apaches.

As the outlaws crossed the Verde River a few miles south of Camp Verde and rode up West Clear Creek Canyon into the higher elevations, King Woolsey and his posse came across the scene of the massacre at Tonto Creek. In a short time, the Pima scouts noted that superimposed over the tracks of the fleeing white men were those of some twenty Apaches. The Pima tracker told Woolsey they were gaining on the bandits.

After entering Willow Valley, Tice determined that the overworked stock could go no further, and decided to camp for the night. The following morning, as the men crawled from their bedrolls, the Apaches who had been following them attacked.

Under a hail of arrows, the bandits alternately returned fire, saddled their horses, and repacked the gold onto the mules. As they rode out of the valley, the Indians pursued, harassing the outlaws from their flanks. Tice wanted to make a stand and fight off the attackers, but O'Reilly directed the men to a break in the forest that led to a narrow canyon. Here, he reasoned, they would be able to hold off the Indians. After arriving, they found that the canyon was only two hundred yards long, and there was no way out except the way they rode in. They pulled the heavy loads from the animals and turned them loose to graze on the grasses that grew on the floor of the canyon.

In the dark of night, two of the bandits managed to escape from the canyon on foot. Nothing is known of their fate, but many believe the Apaches caught and killed them. The next day, Tice and the others realized they were low on food and ammunition and would not be able to make a prolonged stand in the canyon. After exploring the upper reaches of the box canyon, Tice discovered a possible way out. It would entail carving a trail up one of the canyon slopes. When he showed it to his companions, they argued against it, claiming it was too risky. Tice explained it was either that or face the vengeance-minded Apaches waiting for them at the mouth of the canyon.

Following some discussion, it was decided that Tice and O'Reilly would take two of the strongest horses up the trail. If they made it to the top, they would ride to the trading post at Horsehead Crossing on the Little Colorado River. Here, they would procure supplies and extra men and return for the others.

After making the difficult escape from the canyon, the two men spurred their horses toward Horsehead Crossing. The prolonged flight was too much for the mounts. At the end of the first day, they both collapsed and were unable to continue. Tice and O'Reilly continued on foot. When they finally arrived at Frayde's Trading Post, they were welcomed by the owner. Though he provided the two men with abundant whiskey for the two days they took to recover, he had no ammunition or food in stock. He directed them to Holbrook, a young town thirty miles to the east that was destined to be a stop on the expanding railroad. Frayde sold the two men a pair of stout horses, for which he was paid from some of the proceeds of the Shawnix Station robbery.

On arriving at Holbrook, Tice and O'Reilly purchased the necessary supplies and attempted to enlist some men to return with them. Any available men worked for high wages paid by the Atlantic and Pacific Railroad Company and refused to travel into dangerous Apache country. On the fifth day after riding out of the canyon, the two men set out to return to their companions.

The same morning Tice and O'Reilly left Holbrook, the five men remaining in the canyon despaired of their return. Having exhausted their already meager food supplies, they were forced to kill one of the horses and cook its meat. During the five days they were in the canyon, they worked at widening the trail that led up the dangerous slope. In addition, the time in the canyon allowed the horses and mules much-needed rest. Just before noon, the men loaded up all of the gold and remaining supplies on the horses and mules and rode to the safety of the rim above.

As the outlaws rode out of the canyon, King Woolsey and his posse came up behind the Apaches guarding the entrance to the canyon. Seeing the futility of fighting new and heavily armed aggressors with bows and arrows, the Indians retreated into the woods. With no resistance,

W. C. JAMESON

Woolsey led his men into the canyon. A thorough inspection revealed no outlaws. One of the trackers showed Woolsey the trail up by which the outlaws had escaped. Anxious to make up for lost time, they rode up the path and were again soon on the trail of the bandits.

Riding as fast as their overloaded horses would allow, the three outlaws followed a trail that led toward Buck Mountain. On nearing the prominence, the trail swung east and skirted the southern flank. At this point, the three encountered Tice and O'Reilly returning from Holbrook. They first thing they asked for was food, so they rode a short distance off the trail. Without unsaddling and unloading the animals, they built a fire and prepared a quick meal. Unknown to them, the Apaches had picked up their trail a short time after they had left the canyon and were only minutes away.

When the bandits were halfway through their meal, the Indians struck again, firing arrows into the midst of the outlaws from the concealment of the trees. Dropping their plates, the outlaws scrambled onto their horses and, leading the pack mules, rode away toward the east. For two hours they pushed the animals hard until James called to Tice that his horse had gone lame. Several dozen yards off the trail was a limestone cliff. Along the base were several shallow shelter caves. It was toward these that Tice led the party.

This time the outlaws shucked the packs of gold and the saddles from the exhausted horses and mules and carried their fortune into one of the caves. Moments after James pulled the saddle off his horse, the animal fell to the ground, dead. The weary men retreated to the shade of one of the caves as their horses and mules grazed just beyond the entrance.

Within an hour, the Apaches arrived and launched another attack. The surprised outlaws were caught with their guard down, and in the ensuing skirmish, two of them were killed. In addition, three horses and two of the mules were shot dead with dozens of arrows.

By the time the surviving outlaws retrieved their guns and began returning fire, the Indians had vanished. Tice suggested they were preparing for another attack. He was correct. Minutes later, the Apaches materialized from behind trees and boulders and launched more arrows into the cave. This time, the outlaws turned away the attack, killing several Apaches in the process. After the Indians retreated into the forest, Tice, James, and an unnamed outlaw retrieved the packs containing the gold, along with the barrel of blasting powder, caps, and fuses, and carried them into the cave.

Two hours before sundown, the Apaches launched another attack. Just as the three outlaws opened fire on the Indians, Woolsey and his posse arrived and struck the Indians from the rear. After losing several braves to the bullets of the white men, the Indians once again faded away.

After surveying the scene, Woolsey, taking cover behind a large rock, called out to the outlaws to surrender. Receiving no answer, he wondered if they had all been killed by the Apaches. Cautioning his men to be careful, he instructed them to approach the cave, taking cover as they went. To make certain no escape attempt was made, Woolsey shot the remaining horses and mule.

Just as the sun was only minutes away from dropping below the horizon, gunfire erupted from within the cave. Return fire from the posse killed two more of the outlaws, leaving only Tice and O'Reilly. The older man told Tice that he was going to set a charge and blow the cave ceiling down over the treasure. After escaping from the posse, he told his friend, they could return later and dig it out.

While Tice kept the posse at bay with his precise shooting, O'Reilly set the charge. Just before it was set to blow, Tice crawled out of the shelter under cover of darkness and began making his way along the edge of the cliff, away from the posse. He was joined by James, who had been hiding in a different cave. Before O'Reilly was able to join them, he was gunned down. As he lay dying on the floor of the cave, an explosion ripped the night, and the roof collapsed onto the outlaw and the $400,000 in gold. Tice and James took advantage of the distraction and, in a low crouch, they escaped unnoticed from the scene.

Woolsey waited until ten o'clock, when the full moon was up, to advance toward the cave. Shooting as they went, the posse members experienced no return fire. Presently, Woolsey called a cease-fire and inspected the area. He found the bodies of the dead outlaws and presumed the rest were buried under the rocks loosened by the blast.

At dawn, Woolsey searched for the gold the bandits had carried. He was unaware that it was buried beneath the collapse in the small cave. He assumed that a bullet from one of his men had struck a powder keg, causing the explosion. When he did not find the gold, he returned to the box canyon and searched there. Having no luck, he disbanded the

W. C. JAMESON

posse and returned to his Salt Valley ranch. King Woolsey died one month later.

Two days following their escape from Woolsey's posse, at dusk, Tice and James arrived once again at Frayde's trading post. The helpful owner took them in, fed them, and provided them with enough supplies to get them to Holbrook. In spite of traveling around much of Arizona with a fortune in gold, the two men had no money in their pockets and were forced to seek employment. At Holbrook, they landed jobs working on the railroad.

As Tice and James worked their jobs, they made friends with Peter Brogdon and Adolphus Pierce. In time, Tice told them about the $400,000 in gold lost under a collapse of rocks near Buck Mountain. He did not tell them it was stolen. As soon as he and O'Reilly had set aside enough money to pay for horses and supplies, he explained, they were going back after it. He invited Brogdon and Pierce to go along. By the time tracks had been laid from Holbrook to Winslow, thirty-five miles to the west, Tice and James had enough money to supply an expedition to retrieve the gold. Leaving James, Brogdon, and Pierce at Winslow, Tice hitched a ride to Frayde's trading post, a short distance from Winslow. Here, he purchased horses, food, and equipment.

In Winslow, James got into a poker game. During an argument, he was shot by a professional gambler. Bleeding badly, he was carried by an acquaintance to a cabin and was soon joined by Brogdon and Pierce. In between bouts of delirium, James confessed to robbing the stagecoach and the Shawnix Station. Brogdon and Pierce were stunned to discover their new friends were outlaws. James died that night.

Midmorning of the following day, Tice returned with the horses and supplies. When told of his friend's death and the cause of it, he loaded his revolver and went in search of the gambler. Just past noon, he found him in a saloon and emptied his handgun into the gambler's chest, killing him. Before Tice could leave, he was jumped by bystanders and held until the sheriff could arrive. The next day he was taken to the county jail at St. Johns, eighty miles to the southeast.

During his incarceration, Tice made friends with his jailer, who in turn introduced him to Nat and Dick Greer—two men known for their outlaw ways, but who had never been caught. The Greer brothers secured a lawyer for Tice and paid him a retainer. In return for their generosity, Tice told them about the $400,000 in gold near Buck Mountain. When the lawyer told Tice that he would likely be found guilty and sentenced to hang, the prisoner began to make other plans and summoned the Greer brothers to help him.

One evening a week later, after the guard was changed, Tice produced a gun and forced the jailer to unlock the cell. After tying up the guard, Tice walked out the front door of the jail, where he expected to find a saddled horse waiting for him. He was recognized by a group of citizens passing by at that moment. They realized a jailbreak was in progress, pulled their weapons, and shot Tice dead on the spot.

Days later, the Greer brothers went in search of the gold, relying on the meager directions provided by Tice. When interviewed years later, Dan Greer said they arrived in the region indicated by Tice and encountered an unbroken wilderness of valleys, canyons, cliffs, and boulders. After a cursory search, they gave up and returned to St. Johns. Brogdon and Pierce also made an attempt to find the gold, but had no luck.

In 1890, a professional treasure hunter named George McCormick decided to undertake a search for the gold. He received a set of directions from a man who had gotten them from Brogdon. McCormick checked records and verified the robbery of the stagecoach and the Shawnix Station. He also made a trip to the Buck Mountain area and found a cliff face with a number of shallow caves at the base. During preparations for a second trip to the area, McCormick received an offer to serve as superintendent of mines for a company located at Flagstaff. The offer was a good one, and he decided the search for the treasure would have to be delayed for a time.

It was not until 1921 that McCormick was able to return to the search for the lost gold. Accompanied by his son, Melvin, he returned to Buck Mountain. In addition to the cave-pocked cliff face he had encountered on his first trip, he found at least three more sections of cliff containing caves. Though his search continued for the next twenty years, McCormick never found the treasure.

In 1947, a power-line contractor was boring test holes not far from Buck Mountain preparatory to setting up a series of power-line towers. The cores were collected and weeks later examined. One day, while recording his observations of the core of one particular hole, he found a piece of solid gold the thickness of a brick. The gold had been smelted and poured into a mold. On the top portion of the core was stamped a "J." Clearly, the drill had cut through an ingot buried close to the surface.

W. C. JAMESON

The contractor knew of George McCormick and his search for lost treasure in the area, so he contacted him. McCormick, now an old man, examined the piece of gold and concluded it came from an ingot manufactured at the Ajo mine. The only way it could have arrived at the location where it was found was if it had been dropped by a member of the Tice gang. McCormick wondered if it might have been part of the loot that was lost while the bandits were taking shelter in the cave. When McCormick requested the location of the discovery, the contractor explained that all of the records had been lost. Ultimately, the power lines were constructed a significant distance from where the initial cores were taken.

In 1964, Lester Perkins, who had acquired knowledge of the Tice Gang's lost gold, loaded a pack mule and rode into the region near Buck Mountain in order to conduct a search. After finding a number of vertical cliffs with small caves associated with them, he concentrated on one in particular and was rewarded with the discovery of one small opening that had suffered a cave-in. Perkins concluded that it was not a natural collapse, and that only a strong blast could have accomplished such a thing. He set up camp and began the laborious task of removing the debris. For days he labored. Sometimes he was forced to cut thick limbs to employ as levers and pry some of the larger rocks out of the opening. One afternoon he discovered a rotted pack saddle that had been buried under the collapse. Another two days of work yielded pieces of bridle fittings, a portion of a charred saddle, and a handgun. Perkins was certain he had found the location of the buried gold.

His food stores had run low, and Perkins was forced to abandon the site to replenish supplies. He packed out of the area and returned to his home in Superior. With great excitement, he told his wife what he had found and that within a week he would return to the cave to retrieve the gold. Two days later, Perkins died from a heart attack. He left no map or directions to his discovery.

It has been estimated that the $400,000 worth of gold taken by the Tice Gang in 1879 would be worth close to $50,000,000 today. The possibility of such wealth continues to lure the adventurous and the hopeful into the region of Buck Mountain. The treasure, however, remains elusive.

GRAND
CANYON
CARDENAS
HOPI
LITTLE COLORADO
TIERRA
COLORADO
RIVER
GILA RIVER
DIAZ
ZUNI
ACOMA
TIGU
X
El Paso
RIO
ARIZPE
CORAZONES II
CORAZONES I
RIO SONORA
CHIHUAHUA
RIO YAQUI
VACAPA
RIO MAYO
RIO FUERTE
PETATLAN
RIO SINALOA
MOCORITO
TOPIA
CULIACAN

Southeast

The Lost Dutchman Gold
of the Superstition Mountains

Of all the famous tales and legends of lost mines and buried treasure in North America, few have received as much attention or have
captured the imagination of the public as the so-called Lost Dutchman
Mine of the Superstition Mountains. It has likely been written about
more than any other and is among the most controversial stories. With
the passage of so much time, it is difficult to separate legend from fact.
Located somewhere deep in the forbidding Superstition Mountains east
of Phoenix, this legendary source of gold has tantalized researchers and
treasure hunters for well over a century.

The Superstition Mountains are an appropriate setting for this intriguing tale of lost gold. At one time a remote rattlesnake-infested
Apache homeland of rocky canyons, sharp ridges, and steep slopes,
these mountains remain among the most rugged, arid, and tortuous in
the American Southwest.

Long before this region was visited by gold-seeking Spaniards during the early sixteenth century, the local Indians believed the range to
be inhabited by a number of special gods who protected the gold found
therein. A Thunder God, who supposedly viewed the Superstitions as
his kingdom, had the power to roll rocks from the high cliffs onto any
who dared enter the region to take the gold. It was from this Indian legend that the so-called Curse of the Superstition Mountains was derived.

The Pima Indians were the source of another legend. They believed
that when the Aztec ruler Montezuma gathered up his followers and
his great fortune, he traveled from deep in Mexico into the Superstition
Mountains. Here, it is said, he buried uncountable millions of dollars

worth of gold, silver, and jewels. Montezuma judged it would be safe from raiders in this remote natural sanctuary.

Spanish explorers under the command of Coronado entered the region during the early 1500s. In 1539, one particular expedition, led by Fray Marcos de Niza, set forth from Mexico City to locate a quantity of gold believed to exist somewhere in the vast region to the north. He took along geologists, miners, and engineers. As a result of de Niza's observations and deductions, the Spaniards undertook prospecting and mining operations throughout much of this new country. Gold and silver were discovered in numerous locations, and hundreds of mines were established. Several shaft and placer mines were opened in the Superstition Mountains, all yielding great quantities of gold as well as silver. For several generations, the Spaniards successfully extracted precious ore from this range. The gold was processed, formed into ingots, and accumulated. Every two or three months, pack trains, each transporting hundreds of the ingots, plied the hazardous trails from the mines to Mexico City far to the south.

As the Spanish mining activity in the Superstitions increased, so did the Apache resentment of the intruders. These Indians had long considered the Superstitions to be their homeland and holy ground, and they grew concerned about the growing encroachment of the newcomers. In addition, in their quest for food, the Spanish hunters were decimating herds of deer and buffalo to the degree that little remained for the Indians. In time, the Apaches grew frustrated and retaliated. At first, small parties of hunters were ambushed along the narrow trails. As the ranks of the Spaniards were slowly thinned, the Indians began attacking the mining camps. Daylong battles often ensued, with the Spanish always getting the worst of it.

The Spanish continued to work the rich mines until the mid-1700s, when they began the gradual process of abandoning the area. In some cases, they left because they had depleted the ore. In others, it was because of the unrelenting Indian depredations. Mining activity in the Superstitions eventually ceased altogether. Before leaving, the Spaniards covered all of the entrances to the shafts in the hope that this would deter any who followed them into the mountain range, and they planned to be able to return and resume their operations one day.

For several years the Superstitions lay relatively quiet and undisturbed. No more could the ring of pickaxes and the sounds of men be heard. Few but the Apache Indians passed through this area, and they remained constantly on guard against the return of the Spanish miners. Unknown to the Indians at the time, the Mexican Revolution of 1821 marked the end of Spanish reign in the region, thus prohibiting them from returning to extract more of the gold, much of which remained in the mountains.

Years later in Mexico, a man named Peralta learned of the rich gold mines located far to the north that the Spaniards had been forced to abandon. For years, the Peralta family had operated several successful gold mines in the Mexican state of Sonora as well as southern Arizona, and consequently became intrigued by the possibility of extending their interests into the Superstition Mountains. After obtaining geographical, geological, and engineering information on the Superstition mines that were left behind by the Spanish government, Don Miguel Peralta II organized a party to travel to the isolated and still dangerous range with the hope of locating gold and reopening the shafts. Not only did Peralta employ laborers, geologists, and engineers, he also hired dozens of guards for protection against marauding Indians. By the time the expedition left Mexico for the Superstition Mountains, it numbered over four hundred.

As it turned out, digging gold from the Superstitions was as profitable for Peralta as it had been for the Spaniards. But during the 1840s, Peralta, now in his sixties, learned of the impending Treaty of Hidalgo, which would eventually grant this part of Mexico to the United States. The treaty was to take effect in 1848, so Peralta hurried to extract as much gold as he could prior to being forced off the land.

On arriving at the range, the Peralta expedition, using the Spanish maps, relocated several placer mines and reopened some of the more productive shafts. They worked as long as eighteen hours a day in order to accumulate as much gold as possible in the relatively short amount of time they had remaining. In addition to the impending deadlines of the treaty, the Peralta expedition also had to contend with growing numbers of Apache Indians. Miners, hunters, and guards occasionally fell victim to Indian arrows, and talk of the Curse of the Superstition Mountains occupied the conversations of the Spaniards.

As the time to leave the area approached, like the Spaniards before him Peralta had all of the mines covered and camouflaged, believing this would serve as a deterrent to others who might be interested in the gold—for he hoped that someday he might be able to make the appropriate political arrangements to return and extract more of the rich ore that lay in the shafts. After having tons of gold loaded onto mules, Peralta transported his new wealth back into Mexico via a series of pack trains. Because of limited time and the abundance of gold, he was forced to bury millions of dollars worth of it in secret locations not far from the shafts.

One such pack train consisting of twenty mules, each carrying heavy leather sacks filled with gold ore and led by a contingent of armed and mounted guards, wound its way through the canyons and out of the range toward a road to Mexico City. As mules and guards passed single-file along a narrow trail that paralleled Camp Creek in the Superstition Mountains, they were ambushed by Apaches.

The guards bolted in panic, only to be overtaken and slaughtered by the Indians. After the milling and excited mules were rounded up, the Indians cut the packs away and scattered the gold in the creek bed. The mules, on the other hand, were considered a delicacy, a favored meat among the members of the tribe. Aside from the occasional use to make ornaments such as armbands and necklaces, the Apaches cared little for the metal.

To this day, hikers along Camp Creek are still able to find gold nuggets in and near this ephemeral stream.

The Treaty of Hidalgo was signed in 1848 at almost the same time gold was discovered in California. The two events were to work together to eventually link Peralta to a German immigrant named Jacob Walz (also spelled Waltz and Waltzer), who would become a prominent figure associated with the lost gold of the Superstition Mountains.

Walz arrived on North American shores with considerable mining experience, which he put to use almost immediately at gold strikes in North Carolina and Georgia. He was living in Mississippi when he learned about the great gold discoveries in California. Along with thousands of others during that time, he packed his bags and headed west with the intention of becoming rich. Little is known of Walz's somewhat reclusive activities before 1860, but it is believed he worked several small and ultimately unproductive placer claims in northern California. It was here he became known as the Dutchman, a nickname that stuck with him for the rest of his life.

According to legend, one evening while he was enjoying a beer in a tavern in some small mining town, Walz was distracted by a disturbance.

W. C. JAMESON

Near the opposite end of the bar, an angry gambler was beating on an elderly and unarmed man. Just as the gambler plunged a knife into the stomach of the defenseless man, Walz stepped in and disarmed the protagonist. He then carried the bleeding victim to his room at a nearby hotel, treated his wound, and over the next few days nursed him back to health. While a guest in Walz's hotel room, the old man introduced himself as Don Miguel Peralta II, and the two became friends. When Peralta recovered, he told Walz about his rich gold mines in the Superstition Mountains of Arizona. At first Walz did not believe Peralta, but the old man provided him with directions and a map.

Around the same time that the War Between the States was gaining momentum in the South, Walz, using the directions given to him, made his way to the Superstition range to look for the mines. He had difficulty interpreting Peralta's map, but after several years of searching, finally found gold. In the western end of the range near the normally dry Camp Creek, Walz found much of the ore scattered earlier by the Apaches during their raid, along with a significant placer deposit. Nearby, he located the ruins of several rock houses in which miners and guards once lived. Not far from those, he found two shafts that had been covered over. From where he stood near these shafts, Walz could see a sharply pointed peak to the south that a number of researchers have identified as Weavers Needle, a prominent landmark. Other investigators are convinced that Walz was looking at Pinnacle Peak. After exploring the region for several days, Walz found several large caches of gold ore and ingots that had been buried by Peralta.

Once Walz determined that he had found Peralta's mining claim, he bent to the task of panning ore from several of the small streams and reopening the mine shafts. As he panned and dug gold, he allegedly cached large quantities of it alongside Peralta's stashes and at other places. Apparently, the only time he ever left the range was to travel to Phoenix to purchase supplies.

While in town, Walz paid for his goods with gold nuggets—the purest ever seen in the region, according to many. When townspeople inquired about the source of the gold, Walz was always heard to exclaim that no one would ever find his mines. He soon became known locally as the Dutchman, and was greeted as such when he arrived in town.

As more and more people became acquainted with Walz's mining successes, some began following him on his return trips to the Superstitions.

Walz suspected as much and easily eluded his trackers. Several men who had set out on the Dutchman's trail were never seen again, and it was believed that Walz likely waited in ambush and killed them. Such tales added to the growing mystery about the Curse of the Superstitions.

Walz extracted gold from the mines for twenty years. As he grew older, his health began to fail and various infirmities took their toll. During his last few years in the range, Walz dropped hints relative to the location of the mines, but he shared precise directions with only one person, a woman he had befriended years earlier. Her name was Julia Thomas; she owned an ice-cream parlor in Phoenix and was one of the few black women in the area. Most believe the directions Walz provided Thomas were generally accurate, for he would have had no reason to deceive her. Paraphrased, his directions are as follows:

> Follow the Salt River from Phoenix until arriving at a junction with a well-traveled trail. Take the trail to Sombrero Peak, and from this point continue to the Eye of the Needle [which many today believe to be Pinnacle Peak]. From the eye, the mines lie almost due north. Continue to Blacktop Hill, thence to Blacktop Mesa. On the mesa can be seen an old stone corral left by the Spaniards. Cross the mesa and continue down the opposite side where a spring can be seen. Follow the trail northward until coming to another spring. Beyond this spring lies a canyon, and the mines are located at the head of it.

Walz also told Thomas that placer gold could be found at various locations in the dry streambed that ran along the canyon floor. An entrance to one important shaft was on the north-facing slope near the head of the canyon. Walz explained that one could stand as close as ten feet to the opening of the mine and still not see it. Inside was an eighteen-inch-thick vein of almost pure gold. Standing in front of the opening, one could see the ruins of an old rock house originally constructed by the Spaniards. At the top of the slope beyond the rock house was another shaft, this one vertical and containing a thick seam of gold.

Other directions to Walz's gold exist, many of them cobbled together from the hints he dropped during his trips to town. Some, of course, are purely hoaxes, and most contradict one another.

Jacob Walz died in 1891 in the home of Julia Thomas. With his death

W. C. JAMESON

came the growing, often exaggerated tales of his gold. As a result, numerous expeditions entered the Superstition Mountains in search of what came to be called the Lost Dutchman Mine, though instead of a single mine there exist several shafts, placer deposits, and caches. From that time to today, hundreds of quests have been launched to find the fabled sources of the gold. Dozens of men have lost their lives. Many were the victims of Apache attacks, and others perished from thirst, snakebite, exposure, and falls from cliffs. All of those who died were believed to be victims of the curse.

Today, there exist dozens of books and thousands of articles about the Lost Dutchman Mine, and several movies have been made on the subject—all of which add to the legend. Despite all of the attention given to this tale, the sources of the gold have remained lost. Some contend that the mine shafts were hidden again by the Dutchman before he died; others suggest they were covered by landslides generated by an earthquake in 1877. Many have argued that the gold was simply depleted as a result of the mining activities of the Spaniards, Peralta, and Walz. And some will tell you that perhaps it never existed at all.

That the Spaniards found gold in the Superstition Mountains cannot be denied, for it is a matter of historical record. The same can be said for the huge mining operations undertaken by Don Miguel Peralta II. That Jacob Walz found gold in the range is an established fact. Others have claimed to have found the rich placers and shafts, but subsequent investigations have revealed such announcements to be hoaxes.

The truth is, the canyon containing the old mine shafts and the placers has been found by subsequent prospectors and treasure hunters. While there is abundant evidence of extensive mining of what may have been a large amount of gold, and possibly the depletion of the source, the fact remains that the caches secreted both by Peralta and Walz have not yet been found. These continue to lure the hopeful into the Superstition Mountains.

Doc Thorne's
Lost Gold Mine

Next to the Dutchman Gold of the Superstition Mountains, the most talked about, and likely the most searched for, lost mine in Arizona is that of Doc Thorne. There is little doubt that the magnificent source of gold existed; though men have searched for over one hundred years, it remains lost.

In 1852, Doc Thorne, in the company of seven other men, left California heading east. Their objective and destination is not known. What is known, however, is that on arriving at the stagecoach station at Maricopa Wells in Arizona, they were attacked by Apaches. Following the brief battle, only Thorne and a man named Brown survived. They were taken captive by the Indians and transported to their village in the Mazatal Mountains, about eighty miles northeast of Phoenix. Here, they were put to work as slaves. The Apaches lived in a semipermanent encampment composed of brush wickiups, not far from a tributary of the Salt River. The well-hidden camp was located near the base of a low mountain. The trail that led to it was difficult and wound over rough volcanic rock.

From time to time, a party of warriors would ride from the camp to conduct raids on area settlers and travelers. During these times, Thorne and Brown were left in the village to do the bidding of the women. On these occasions, the two white men were permitted to move freely about the encampment. Knowing that the small village was a long way from succor, and that he would have to make his way unarmed and naked across an arid, hostile desert in search of it, Thorne did his best to remain contented with his lot.

Not so his partner. One night, Brown crept from the encampment and out into the wild land beyond. It was the last Thorne saw of him, and his fate remains a mystery. Thorne continued to haul firewood and water, helped skin animals, and performed other chores. He knew that someday the opportunity to escape would arrive, and when it happened he would take full advantage.

Thorne remained with the Apaches for several years. During that time, they came to trust him and were impressed with his ability to work all day without complaint. In addition, Thorne, a physician, treated a variety of sicknesses among the women and children of the tribe. Over time, this endeared him even more to the Indians. Gradually, his status as a slave changed to that of a guest medicine man.

With time, Thorne found himself desiring to return to civilization as he remembered it. His longing to be with his own prompted him to consult with the tribal leaders about allowing him his freedom. They told him they would hold council on the matter and let him know.

The council members agreed that Thorne had been trustworthy and helpful during his captivity and offered no difficulties, as did other slaves. They also regarded him as a beneficial member of the tribe, having provided his skills in treating the sick and wounded. Because of that, they were reluctant to grant him his freedom. In the end, they decided to place the matter in the hands of their chief, Mangas Coloradas.

The chief stated that it was time to give Thorne his freedom. In making this decision, however, Mangas Coloradas also told the members of the tribe that they were not to provide Thorne with a horse, provisions, or water. While a free man, Thorne still was without the capacity to leave the encampment.

Thorne thanked the Indians for granting him his freedom and told them he understood the stipulations. He continued to live among them and perform his medical duties as needed.

During the years Thorne remained with the Apaches, he noticed that from time to time, a warrior would arrive in camp with a pouch or two of gold nuggets from some distant location. The gold, almost pure, was hammered into crude ornaments sometimes worn by the women. Now and then, he heard talk among the tribe that the white men would trade rifles and ammunition for the shiny metal. Over the years he lived with the Indians, Thorne grew convinced that the mine from which they gleaned the gold was a rich one.

The doctor occasionally inquired about the gold and its source, but each time he was told that the location was a secret, that only a few of the elder members knew the location, and that it was forbidden to release the knowledge to one outside of the tribe. Furthermore, they told him, white men were not to be trusted with such information. Thorne respected their need for secrecy and ceased broaching the topic. Still, he remained curious.

Then one day, much to Thorne's surprise, a contingent of warriors approached him and told him that in gratitude for the help he had provided the tribe over the years, they would lead him to the secret gold mine and allow him to fill his pockets with nuggets.

On the appointed day, weeks later, Thorne was provided with a good pony. Explaining the need for secrecy, they placed a blindfold on the doctor and helped him mount. The pony was ridden in a clockwise circle one dozen times, then reversed an equal number in order to confuse the rider.

For several hours, Thorne, astride his mount, was led along a rough, rocky, and winding trail that in places was very steep. After several hours, the party halted and the blindfold was removed.

Thorne looked about. He was in a narrow canyon. The walls were granite. The Apaches directed his gaze to a vein of white quartz only a few feet away. The vein, according to Thorne, was eighteen inches wide; it ran across the floor of the canyon and several feet up an adjacent wall. Within the quartz shone large flecks of bright gold. Here and there, Thorne could see where the quartz had been broken so that the ore could be retrieved by those who came to harvest it. So rich was the deposit that one had only to pluck the gold from the matrix.

Surreptitiously, Thorne glanced around in search of landmarks. His intention was to return to this location someday and dig a fortune from the quartz. From where he stood on the canyon floor, he could look up to the low canyon ridges. Beyond one of them, he could discern the ragged silhouette of four peaks outlined against the sky. Given the narrow confines of the canyon and not knowing the location of the sun, Thorne could not tell in which direction he was looking.

After a moment, one of the Apaches told Thorne he could take a few minutes and fill his pockets with as much gold as he could dig from the quartz. In a short time he had gathered all he could carry. The Indians replaced the blindfold, helped him onto his pony, and rode out of the canyon.

W. C. Jameson

More months passed, and Thorne was able to convince the Indians that he should have a horse. They provided him with one. Each day, he hoarded a bit of his food rations, placing dried meat and bits of bread into a small pack he fashioned from scraps of hide. In the manner of the Apaches, he cleaned a portion of intestine and used it to carry water. One morning he tied these items to his horse, bade the Indians goodbye, and rode away.

Days later, Thorne rode into a small settlement and reunited with white men. He gradually returned to the civilization he knew, though he seldom spoke of his time with the Apaches. He returned to his profession of physician and made a decent living, but his thoughts seldom strayed from the rich vein of gold lying in some unnamed canyon in southwestern Arizona.

In time, the U.S. Army increased the number of troops assigned to the region, and following a number of bitter battles, the Apaches were finally subdued. Once it was deemed safe to reenter the wilderness, Doc Thorne resigned from the medical profession and undertook a search for the gold he was convinced waited for him.

On his first expedition into the region where he had once lived with the Apaches, Thorne located the four peaks he had seen from the floor of the canyon where he stood next to the rich vein. From the four peaks, he ranged out in different directions in hopes of finding the narrow canyon. Thorne made dozens of trips and examined scores of canyons. Those times when he thought he was in the canyon of gold, he was never able to find the location.

After years of failed searches, Doc Thorne decided to give up. A week after returning from an expedition to the Mazatal Mountains, he admitted he had grown too old and feeble to be riding into the wilderness any longer. A few days later, he died in his sleep.

The story of Doc Thorne's lost gold and the wealth that awaited the fortunate finder spread throughout the Southwest. Soon, treasure hunters from around the country arrived in the region. Many entered the remote mountain ranges never to be seen again. Others remained for months, even years, but ultimately admitted failure and departed.

Theories abound concerning the location of Doc Thorne's rich gold mine. Some researchers are convinced, on the basis of comments dropped by the doctor himself, that the rich seam of gold lies in a small canyon located in the White Mountains not far from the Black River.

Others insist that the canyon is farther to the southwest, less than a day's ride from the confluence of the Salt and Verde rivers.

One searcher claimed he had found the vein of gold in a narrow canyon located just south of the confluence of the Black and White rivers in the Mazatal Mountains. The man brought pouches of gold nuggets he said he dug from the quartz vein to an assayer in Phoenix. The tests showed the gold was very rich, but the finder was never able to retrace his steps to the discovery.

To this day, searchers arrive at various locations in southeastern Arizona, each convinced they will be the one to find the lost gold of Doc Thorne. Thus far, it continues to elude them.

The Huachuca
Canyon Treasure

During the months leading up to World War II, Robert Jones served as an enlisted man in a communications division at Fort Huachuca, a remote military installation located in the desert of southeastern Arizona in Cochise County. For several days in a row during one June, the temperatures soared to over one hundred degrees. Air conditioning was nonexistent in those days, and residents scrambled to seek relief from the heat in a variety of ways.

Jones decided to spend his next day off hiking and exploring in the cool, shaded oak and pine environs of the nearby Huachuca Mountains. He invited a friend to accompany him, and together they drove into Huachuca Canyon along an old, seldom-used dirt road, eager for the weekend diversion from their normal duties at the military post.

The men arrived at a point where the road had washed out, making progress difficult. They parked the car and continued on foot up the canyon along the shadowed trail. They heard the calls of blue jays high in the trees. They watched as the birds flew from branch to branch, their screeches sounding an alert to the other denizens of the forest. Squirrels twittered and played in the canopy. Along the trail, the men took care to watch for the ubiquitous rattlesnakes that lived in the area.

As the two friends walked up the canyon, Jones noted with curiosity the changes in the color of some rock near the base of the canyon wall. The loose rubble appeared to be talus from a very old mining operation, but he could discern no shaft above the accumulation. Intrigued, he climbed the slope to have a look. As Jones walked along a stretch of the canyon just above the scree, the ground suddenly gave way and he dropped thirty-two feet into a hidden, nearly vertical shaft.

Stunned and shaken but only slightly injured, Jones called out to his companion. By the time he arrived, Jones realized he had fallen into a steeply slanted mine shaft, one that had apparently been covered over at some long-ago time. From where he sat at the bottom of the drop, he saw that the shaft leveled off and continued laterally into the bedrock of the mountain. Responding to Jones's request, the friend dropped down a tiny flashlight he carried with him. Pointing the narrow beam ahead of him, Jones followed the passageway for twenty to thirty yards, finally arriving at a large but low-ceilinged rectangular chamber that had been carved into the rock and reinforced with hand-laid stones and mortar. Jones, who was five feet seven inches tall, could barely stand upright in the chamber.

Jones explored the room with help from the dim illumination of the flashlight. Stacked along the walls, he found what he determined were twenty-inch-long bars of gold and silver, at least two hundred of each. He picked up one of the bars and estimated that it weighed close to fifty pounds.

Near the center of the chamber, Jones found two large wooden boxes—each, he said, "as big as three washtubs." One of them was filled to the top with gold nuggets, and the other, half full, contained gold dust. Not far from one of the tubs, Jones found a large glass bottle. He picked it up, examined it in the glow of the flashlight, and realized it contained some sort of message. Carefully, Jones withdrew what he later described as a rolled-up sheepskin that contained Spanish writing and a crude map. Unable to understand any of it, he placed it back into the bottle and returned it to where he had found it.

Jones spent almost an hour in the old mine before the flashlight failed. With great difficulty, and with the help of his friend, he made his way back out of the shaft. Excited, Jones told his friend what he had found inside the mine, describing the great fortune in gold and silver. Together, the two men made plans to return to the site and carry out the treasure with help from some fellow soldiers.

Later that afternoon, when the two soldiers returned to Fort Huachuca, they sought out their company commander and related their experience in the mountains. The captain did not believe a single word of the report and dismissed them immediately. The two enlisted men confided in two other officers, both of whom, like the company commander, were convinced they were making up the tale of treasure. They

W. C. JAMESON

then told their first sergeant, Matt Venable. When Venable was interviewed about the Huachuca Canyon treasure years later, he recalled that both Jones and his friend were excellent soldiers and not known to exaggerate. Venable had made a recommendation to military authorities that they investigate the claim, but no action was ever taken.

Discouraged, Jones and his friend decided to bide their time and wait for the right opportunity to retrieve the gold and silver. The next weekend, they returned to the location and determined that it lay within the boundaries of the military reservation. They covered the opening with logs and branches to keep others from finding it. On a nearby tree, Jones made two slashes. Using a rock hammer, he scraped his initials on a granite boulder one had to pass to get to the opening of the concealed shaft.

Jones and his friend intended to undertake their retrieval operation as soon as possible, and identified digging and mining equipment they thought necessary to complete the task. They spoke often of what they would do with the great treasure once they had possession of it. At night, their dreams were filled with visions of gold.

But it was not to be. A few months later, war was declared, and Jones and his partner were transferred out of southeastern Arizona. Jones went to the Pacific, and his friend was shipped to the African-European theater. The friend was killed within days of arriving at his assignment. Not long afterward, Jones was severely wounded in a skirmish on Wake Island and spent the next several months recovering. The need for continued medical treatment and resulting financial difficulties kept Jones from returning to Huachuca Canyon. Eventually, he was discharged from the army with a small pension. He and his wife moved to Dallas, Texas, where she worked as a nurse at the Dallas Medical Center.

For the next eleven years, Jones was busy with the rehabilitation his wounds required. Despite his efforts, he remained a cripple, grew overweight, and had difficulty getting around. He returned to the Huachuca Mountains several times during that period, but was unable to perform the work necessary to retrieve the treasure. He appealed to the U.S. Army for assistance, but was always informed that he would not be allowed to dig for treasure on a military reservation.

In 1959, Jones was introduced to Major General F. W. Moorman, the Fort Huachuca post commander at the time. Unlike other authorities before him, Moorman believed Jones's story. He examined Jones's military record and found him to be competent and reliable. Moorman arranged to have two military psychiatrists interview and evaluate Jones. Both reported that the subject was likely telling the truth about what he found. With this information, along with other materials supporting Jones's credibility, Moorman approved his application to excavate the shaft in Huachuca Canyon. A period of two weeks was granted for the project.

Jones formed a small company to administer and oversee the excavation, with each member to share in the wealth that was retrieved. On the morning of the first day of the allotted period, the group entered the canyon. The participants followed Jones's halting limp to the large boulder where he had carved his initials eighteen years earlier. He also pointed to the slashes on the nearby tree. Several minutes later, Jones was standing atop the logs and branches and other forest debris he said he had used to cover the opening to the shaft. It was quickly pulled away, and moments later, the men began examining the shaft.

What they found was clearly a man-made shaft, perhaps hundreds of years old, that went downward at a steep angle. They also encountered a major problem. Since Jones had left the area years earlier, part of the shaft had collapsed, filling the entrance with tons of rock. The excavators were now faced with the enormous task of removing huge boulders from the vertical opening. Clearly, their picks and shovels were not equal to the task, so Jones petitioned the army for permission to bring in some heavy equipment. They agreed to do so, but only at his expense.

Since Jones was out of funds, Moorman intervened and ordered a military bulldozer brought to the site. Using the bulldozer, much of the talus was cleared away and the opening of the shaft elongated. Rock debris was removed to a depth of ten feet. At that point, it was discovered that the remainder of the vertical shaft was not only filled with large boulders, but also water, thus making further excavation difficult to impossible. The operation was halted. Before Jones could make alternative plans, the time period for excavation had expired and he was required to evacuate the site.

In September of the same year, Jones and his team returned to Fort Huachuca and were successful in obtaining permission to excavate for the treasure in the shaft. Jones had a drilling rig transported to the location and succeeded in boring a hole into the main chamber where the gold and silver were located. If water was encountered, he reasoned, then it could be pumped out through the hole while the debris filling the entrance shaft was removed. The drill bored deep into the rock and broke through into the chamber where the gold and silver were located. As water pumps were hooked up to generators, two bulldozers attacked the clogged shaft. Jones and his companions grew excited; it was just a matter of time, they believed, before they would be carrying out the gold and silver bars.

Unfortunately, just as another twenty feet of the main entrance shaft was cleared, water began seeping in at an alarming rate. More pumps were brought in, and work continued for the next three days and nights. The work became dangerous, as the seeping water caused minor cave-ins in the old, highly weathered granite. When the safety of the workers became threatened, Jones called off the excavation to consider other strategies.

During this lull in the digging, a professional geologist was called in from Colorado to consult on the project. After examining the excavation, he agreed with Jones that they were digging into a very old, man-made shaft, likely one that had been originally excavated by early Spanish miners. He also declared the site unsafe and recommended that the area be sealed off.

The activity in Huachuca Canyon and the promise of finding a great treasure soon attracted the attention of newspaper and television reporters who arrived to record the progress of the search. When their numbers swelled, military officials imposed security measures. They informed Jones that if his operation was not completed soon, the dig would have to be terminated for safety reasons.

Around this time, a representative of the U.S. Treasury Department arrived on the scene and announced that he was empowered to assume charge of any and all treasure that might be discovered. He told Jones that the government would take possession of 60 percent of any gold and silver found. The 40 percent Jones was entitled to would be taxed.

Two weeks later, a large crane with a clam shovel was brought to the site. The crane was able to remove another five feet of material from the shaft, but then encountered resistance from an exceptionally large boulder wedged tight near the bottom. In order to lessen the resistance, a hole was bored into the rock and then stuffed with an explosive. The resulting blast created more problems than it solved, dislodging tons of adjacent rock and causing it to collapse into the shaft, completely refilling it.

According to the geologist, the chamber containing the gold and silver may have also collapsed.

For almost a week, men and machines labored to remove the additional rock, but all traces of the shaft had been obliterated. Jones was forced to abandon the project. Before leaving, he expressed his gratitude to the military authorities who had permitted him to dig, and suggested that he would return for another attempt after acquiring some additional backing. Army officials, however, informed Jones that under no circumstances would they permit him to dig in Huachuca Canyon again.

In spite of the statement from the military, Jones continued to solicit investors and apply for permission to excavate for the treasure he knew lay under tons of rock and rubble in the old mine. He soon found another ally in the post inspector general, Colonel Ethridge Bacon, who stated his belief that there was an excellent chance that the treasure Jones described existed. Though he made several attempts, Bacon was never able to persuade military authorities to allow Jones another attempt. Two years later, Robert Jones passed away in his sleep at his home in Dallas.

The search for the Huachuca Canyon treasure did not end with the death of Jones. In 1975, the U.S. Army granted permission to Quest Exploration, a California-based treasure-hunting company, to try to reach the lost cache. Quest employed state-of-the-art computerized sensing equipment to determine the location of the chamber described by Jones. During the search, Quest was told by the army that any treasure found would be placed in escrow until all claims for it were settled in a court of law.

The treasure-hunting team spent a week trying to locate the chamber, but finally abandoned the project. They explained that whatever openings or passageways that may have existed had undoubtedly caved in as a result of previous excavation work.

When the Quest Exploration team abandoned the site, the military closed off Huachuca Canyon and forbade access to treasure hunters. During a sweep of the canyon, a military policeman discovered a small, man-made shaft in which were found several ancient digging tools, several Spanish coins, and glassware. When the find was reported, army officers confiscated the items and instructed the policeman to keep it confidential.

The official position of the U.S. Army is that the treasure cache described by Robert Jones does not exist. Unofficially, however, the

W. C. JAMESON

army continued to search for it as late as 1979. During autumn of that year, a squirrel hunter who had frequented Huachuca Canyon for years observed army bulldozers and other heavy equipment attempting to excavate the debris-filled shaft that Robert Jones had fallen into thirty-eight years earlier.

Abundant evidence exists to suggest that Robert Jones did indeed chance upon a great treasure in gold and silver in an old, abandoned mine located in Huachuca Canyon. The mine was presumably operated by the Spanish, who were known to have frequented the area in times past. Evidence also suggests that members of the military were convinced of Jones's assertions, even to the point of organizing their own attempt at recovering the treasure, and investing significant time, energy, equipment, and resources in the project. Subsequent visitors to Huachuca Canyon have observed that despite their efforts, the army has never been able to penetrate the obstacles and enter the underground chamber. From all that can be gleaned from the available sources, it appears that the fabulous Huachuca Canyon treasure has never been recovered. Should that be the case, the fortune in gold and silver still lies there in the ruined shaft, buried under tons of rock and rubble.

Vekol's Buried
   Silver Ingots

Just a few miles north of the old ghost town of Vekol, near Casa Grande in Pinal County, lies a cache of three hundred silver ingots, each one weighing twenty-five pounds. The ingots were buried in 1891 in a shallow excavation made in haste, and likely lie only a few inches below the surface. Depending on the purity of the silver, various estimates place the value of the cache at close to one million dollars.

When John D. Walker left his home in Chicago, Illinois, in 1867, he had little notion that he would become a successful rancher and miner. His friends and acquaintances considered him odd for leaving the safety and promise of the city for an unknown future in what many considered to be the dangerous and hostile lands of sparsely settled Arizona. At the time of his departure, Walker was engaged to marry Elinor Rice, and he promised to return for her as soon as he became established.

Walker could not have guessed that his place in history would be sealed as a result of hiding approximately one million dollars worth of silver ingots in a secret location only a few minutes from his Arizona home. Though the location of the treasure likely lies within only a few short miles of what remains of Vekol, and it has been searched for for more than a century, it has yet to be recovered.

On arriving in Arizona, Walker selected an area to homestead about eight miles north of Tucson. During this time, hostile Indians lived in the area, necessitating the presence of the U.S. Cavalry. Walker was warned repeatedly about the threat posed by the indigenes, but he went about his business with confidence, even employing many of the Indians the government considered a menace.

Within a few months of arriving in the area, Walker married Consuela Arriega, despite remaining engaged to Rice. Arriega was a Mexican who, as a child, had been captured and raised by the Pima Indians. The wedding was performed by a Pima elder in the traditional custom of the tribe. Because of his boldness in settling in Indian territory and taking an Indian bride, Walker's closest Anglo neighbors regarded him as strange and had little to do with him.

Walker's ranch prospered. His management style was rigid, and he used a firm hand with his Indian workers. He was regarded as honest and fair, and he paid them well. But he forbade alcohol on his property, and if any of his ranch hands ever showed up for work drunk, they were dismissed on the spot. If he learned that any of his men had visited a saloon in Tucson, they were fired. Despite his strict approach, his employees, for the most part, were loyal, worked hard, and helped him begin turning an impressive profit in a relatively short time.

One person who surprisingly seemed exempt from Walker's rules was a Papago Indian named Juan José Gradello. Gradello arrived in the region about the same time as Walker, and the two immediately struck up a friendship. The Indian worked occasionally for Walker, but would often get drunk and disappear for a week at a time. Sometimes Gradello would remain in the bunkhouse for days, deciding not to engage in ranch work at all. When he sobered up, Walker's response was one of benign tolerance.

Walker and Gradello were often seen walking together around the ranch for hours, engaged in spirited conversation. Those who came upon them at times claimed the two men were always talking about silver.

When Walker had first arrived in the region, he heard a story about a secret silver mine belonging to the Pima Indians. From this mine, he was told, the Indians harvested the nearly pure ore with which they used to fashion ornaments such as armbands and earrings. The tale, considered a local legend, was for the most part dismissed by the white settlers as nothing more than a fanciful yarn. Prospectors would sometimes arrive from different parts of the country and go in search of the mine, but they never found it. Many never returned. It was said that they met their deaths at the hands of the Indians who guarded the secret location. It was also told that any Pima who revealed the location of the mine would meet with a horrible death. John Walker was vitally interested in this legendary mine, and in spite of the dire warnings, decided that he would try to find it.

Though it was never known for certain, many believed that Gradello knew the location of the silver mine, or at least knew members of the Pima tribe who knew. Whatever the truth, the fact remains that thirteen years after coming to Arizona, Walker was taken by Gradello to a remote location several miles south of the Casa Grande ruins, some fifty miles northwest of Tucson, and shown the source of the Indian silver.

Within days, Walker filed a claim on the site and established a town nearby, which he named Vekol, a Papago word for "grandmother." Joining Walker on the claim papers were Gradello and a man named Peter R. Brady. Walker and Brady are also listed as the cofounders of Vekol. The town became official on February 5, 1880.

A mere three months following the filing of the claim, Gradello sold his share to Walker and Brady. A short time later, Walker had a house constructed specifically for Gradello in the new town of Vekol and next door to his own imposing domicile. As was the case on Walker's ranch, Gradello was somehow exempt from rules and city ordinances, all of which were drawn up by Walker.

Within a year of the filing of the claim, a shaft was sunk into a rich vein of silver to a depth in excess of one hundred feet. Walker and Brady were shipping ore to Kansas City, Denver, and San Francisco and pocketing about $2,000 each month—a large sum of money in those times. One year later, an even larger deposit of silver was located nearby, and the two partners tripled their monthly income. By this time, Vekol had a population of around four hundred, many of whom worked in the mines. Walker, who owned the commercial establishments in the town as well as all of the other buildings, ruled Vekol like a king. The only building he did not own was the house occupied by Gradello.

Walker stayed in contact with his family in Chicago and, oddly, remained engaged to Elinor Rice. In the meantime, his Mexican/Pima wife bore him a daughter they named Juana. During the late winter of 1883, one of Walker's brothers, Lucien, arrived in Vekol. Reportedly, John Walker was not overjoyed at seeing his relative. One month later, Lucien and John bought out Brady's one-third interest in the mine for $65,000. Why Brady sold out for such a modest figure remains a mystery, for the mine was processing more silver than ever at the time. Newspapers of the day reported that the operation was netting approximately $1,500 per day. During the summer of 1884, following the construction of a stamp mill, which crushed the ore into powder, it was reported that the mine had earned $167,807 in a three-month period. By now, Vekol had a hotel, a boardinghouse, a library, a livery stable, a school, two churches, and a population of around eight hundred. Walker forbade the construction of a saloon in the town.

In 1886, William Walker, another brother, showed up in Vekol. John Walker was less happy to see William than he had been to see Lucien three years earlier. William was the youngest, boasted of his expertise at running businesses, and within weeks took control of the silver mining operation as well as the management of the town of Vekol.

John Walker was incensed at the actions of his brothers, but his only response was to sulk and keep to himself, speaking only with Gradello. The Papago suggested that John simply dismiss his brothers and have them thrown out of town, but Walker responded that things were too complicated for such a drastic action. As Walker, angry and fuming, paced back and forth across Gradello's living room, he grabbed his heart, staggered, and was about to fall when his friend caught him.

Walker confessed to his friend that he had been suffering dizzy spells for the previous two days. That evening, Gradello, along with Consuelo, transported Walker by buggy to a doctor's office in Tucson. After remaining hospitalized for several days, Walker was told he had suffered a stroke. The physician recommended that he take a vacation to remove himself from the stress of running the silver mine and dealing with his brothers. Walker agreed. He decided to take Consuelo and his daughter to San Francisco for a few weeks.

Before leaving, Walker returned to Vekol to withdraw $80,000 from his bank. Two days later, he and his family arrived in Los Angeles, where he deposited the money in an account he kept there.

Brothers Lucien and William feigned concern about John's health, but while he was gone they petitioned the federal court in Tucson to name them conservators of his vast estate, claiming he was unfit to see to his business. At the time, Arizona was still a territory and remained under the jurisdiction of the federal government. Following prolonged discussions with officials, Lucien and William convinced the court to grant them their wishes, and further convinced it to order that John Walker be confined to an asylum where qualified medical personnel could determine the extent of his insanity.

Two weeks after arriving in San Francisco, John Walker was seized by U.S. marshals in the lobby of the Palace Hotel. Handcuffed, he was transported to the Hospital for the Insane in Napa. Consuelo and Juana, who had been waiting for Walker in their room, were never notified. After frantically searching for her husband, Consuelo contacted Gradello, who arrived in town two days later. Gradello filed a missing-persons report with the San Francisco police, and following the passage of another two days, was notified of Walker's whereabouts and the circumstances leading up to it. Gradello hired a lawyer, and after a month of deliberations, Walker was released from the hospital under a writ of habeas corpus.

Once freed, Walker returned immediately to Vekol to confront his brothers, but was shocked at the news he received. While he had been away, Lucien and William had had the title to the silver mine transferred to them. In addition, they had been named conservators of all of John's properties in town except for his home. A short time later, Lucien and William moved to Tucson and ran the mine and town in absentia.

During subsequent months, hostilities grew and raged between John and his brothers, their confrontations making news on the front pages of the Tucson newspapers. Once again, Lucien and William petitioned the courts to send John away to an asylum. The request was denied this time on the grounds that he had been deemed competent when he was released from the hospital in Napa. When John filed to have his properties returned to him, however, the federal district court rejected his petition. Lawyers were hired on both sides and the conflict grew.

During one particularly bitter court confrontation in Tucson, the brothers charged that John was incompetent and illegally living with a "squaw." John returned to his home in Vekol in an advanced state of agitation. Following dinner with his family, he went to Gradello's house, but the Indian was not home. John left him a note requesting he contact him the moment he returned. Around midnight, Gradello knocked on Walker's door. John received him and led him into one of the bedrooms. After closing the door, Walker motioned Gradello to the closet. There, stacked under several blankets, were three hundred ingots of silver, each weighing twenty-five pounds.

Walker explained to Gradello that his brothers believed the ingots had been transported to a vault in Tucson, and they were in the process of obtaining a court order to retrieve them in the morning. When they discovered the vault was empty, Walker was certain they would come to the house to search for them. He asked Gradello to obtain a stout wagon

W. C. JAMESON

and a team of strong horses to be used in moving the ingots to a better hiding place.

Within the hour, Walker and Gradello were loading the ingots into a large freight wagon the Papago had secured. Walker informed his friend that he was going to bury the ingots a short distance away and that he did not want him to go along, explaining that if Gradello did not know where the silver was hidden, he would not be able to testify to such knowledge in court.

Gradello noted by his watch that it was two in the morning when Walker drove away in the ingot-filled wagon. The vehicle strained under the heavy load, and Walker took care to drive slowly. Gradello watched as the wagon turned north onto the road that led toward the town of Casa Grande. When his friend had disappeared from sight, Gradello went to the house to remain with Consuelo and Juana.

A few minutes after 4:00 a.m., Walker returned. The wagon was empty. When he was greeted by Gradello, he told his friend that the ingots were hidden "almost in plain sight," but that no one would ever find them.

The following afternoon, Gradello knocked on Walker's door and was greeted by Consuelo. Tearfully, Mrs. Walker told him that John was gone and that he was not coming back. Before leaving, he had his lawyers deed the house over to her, and left word that if she ever needed money, all she had to do was contact him.

On April 18, 1891, John Walker wed Elinor Rice in Tucson; in response to a letter, she had arrived in Arizona only a few days previously. Finally, after a twenty-four-year-long engagement, Rice was married to her betrothed. There is no record that Walker divorced Consuelo. Indeed, there is no record that they were ever officially married, other than oral affirmations relative to the tribal ceremony.

The honeymoon was short-lived. The day after the wedding, Walker was arrested on yet another commitment order obtained by his brothers and placed in the jail in Tucson to await a competency hearing. The new Mrs. Walker summoned attorneys, who convinced the judge that the charge was vindictive and contrived. Walker was turned loose.

Walker's freedom was not to last long. Lucien and William, having discovered the vault empty of the three hundred silver ingots, filed a charge of embezzlement against their brother. Walker spent the night in jail and was released the following day after bail of $50,000 had been posted. The case was brought to trial, and the charges were subsequently dismissed when the court ruled that it was legally impossible to embezzle one's own property.

John Walker was in and out of court many times over the next several days. Each time, lawyers for his brothers asked him of the whereabouts of the three hundred silver ingots. Each time he refused to reveal their location. A judge who had gained the favor of Lucien and William ruled that John Walker would be held in contempt of court unless he revealed the hiding place of the treasure. He refused.

Before Walker could be brought into court again, he suffered another stroke. This time, the brothers were successful in having him committed once again to the Napa Hospital for the Insane. Less than three months later, on July 2, 1891, he died. Elinor Walker, after waiting two and a half decades to join John, was a widow.

On August 3, the body of Consuelo Walker was found by Gradello in her home in Vekol. It was determined that she had died from a heart attack. The child, Juana, was taken by Gradello to raise.

Several weeks later, the courts found that the estate of John Walker was worth $1.5 million. Excluded from this figure were the three hundred silver ingots. With Gradello's help, Juana was named heir, though Lucien and William fought the claim. Elinor Walker was not included in her late husband's will, and it was reported that she returned to Chicago without filing a claim. She was never heard from again.

The fight for Juana's share of her father's fortune remained in the courts for the next seventeen years. By the time lawyers had subtracted their share, little was left, and the remainder was eventually awarded to Lucien and William. Juana was ineligible for the inheritance because the court decreed that the marriage between her white father and Mexican/Indian mother was invalid.

Shortly after the death of John Walker, the silver mine played out, and Vekol began to decline as people moved away. The post office was closed in 1909, and by 1915, no one remained in town. The last person to leave was Gradello.

Over the years, Gradello searched for the buried silver ingots, but to no avail. He reasoned that the trove could not be far from Walker's house. He recalled that Walker was gone for only two hours. It would have taken him at least an hour to excavate a hole, stack the ingots into it, and refill it. That left one hour of travel time, and the last time Gradello saw Walker driving the wagon, he was going very, very slow. So, thirty minutes each way, driving at a snail's pace, could place the hoard as close as two miles north of the ghost town of Vekol, perhaps even closer.

Gradello passed away before locating the hiding place of the silver. He was convinced that Walker buried the ingots in a shallow hole, but others suggest the miner may have stuffed them into a rock crevice. Whatever the case, the silver has remained lost for over a century. Because the tale of John Walker's buried treasure is not widely known, even in Arizona, precious few have searched for it. Given the advancements made in metal detectors in recent years, the likelihood of some patient, knowledgeable treasure hunter with sophisticated equipment finding it increases with each passing week.

Skeleton
Canyon Treasure

During the latter part of the nineteenth century, a gang of bandits conducted a raid on the city of Monterrey in the Mexican state of Nuevo León. During the robbery of the bank, they were confronted by a small contingent of Mexican soldiers and police, and a battle ensued. Several of the soldiers were killed. In addition to the bank, the bandits looted the city's cathedral. Packing their booty onto a number of stout mules, they fled Monterrey, heading northwest toward a remote and seldom-used pass through the mountains near a point where Mexico, New Mexico, and Arizona share a common boundary.

At the time of the robbery, it was estimated that the value of the loot exceeded two million dollars. It consisted of one million dollars worth of diamonds, thirty-nine bars of gold, dozens of bags of gold and silver coins, and an undetermined amount of gold statuary taken from the church. The journey from Monterrey to the pass was almost one thousand winding miles over poor roads. The outlaws were pursued for several days, but the soldiers were no match for their weaponry and marksmanship.

Weeks later when the party crossed the national border into southeastern Arizona, they wound their way through a little-known canyon. Here, intrigue and double cross led to an ambush that resulted in the deaths of at least one dozen men, and the burial of a substantial portion of the treasure. Since then, the pass has been known as Skeleton Canyon, and the buried treasure, estimated to be worth millions today, is still being searched for.

In 1891, a small gang of bandits led by Curly Bill Brocious terrorized stagecoach shipments and travelers in the vicinity of Silver City, New

Mexico. For months the gang plied their outlaw trade, but by the time the spoils of the robberies were divided by the five men, the rewards were slim. Curly Bill wanted to move on to bigger, more lucrative targets, but was unsure of how to go about it.

One evening, the five outlaws met at Curly Bill Brocious's cabin not far from Silver City. The gang members included Jim Hughes, Zwing Hunt, Billy Grounds, and Doc Neal. Several years earlier, Hughes had killed three people during a stagecoach robbery in Texas. He was nearly caught by law-enforcement authorities, but succeeded in escaping across the border into Mexico. He fled to Monterrey, where he lived for a year. During his time there, he grew proficient in the Spanish language and also learned of the various riches to be found in that city.

When Hughes decided to leave Monterrey, he traveled westward, ending up in the Mexican state of Sonora. Here, he fell in with José Estrada, a feared Mexican bandit and killer. Hughes proved to be a hardworking and courageous member of the gang, one of thirty to forty members, and he remained with the bandit leader for several months. Following a series of raids, the Estrada gang was pursued by an army patrol, forcing them to take refuge in the Sierra Madres close to the border with the United States. At this point, Hughes bade his friend goodbye and told him he was going to head back toward home. A short time later, he joined Curly Bill's gang in Silver City.

While Hughes was meeting with Brocious and the other outlaws that evening, he related stories of his time in Mexico, and in particular, Monterrey. Intrigued, Curly Bill suggested they travel to the city and raid it. The other outlaws agreed, eager for the wealth they knew they would realize from such an escapade.

Hughes thought the idea good, but explained that a gang of Anglos riding into the city would arouse suspicion. Besides, he said, five men were not enough. They needed a small army. Then he offered an idea. He would contact his friend Estrada and enlist his aid in conducting the robbery. He would tell Estrada that disposing of the loot in Mexico would be a problem, and that if he transported it to the United States, he and Brocious would arrange for its exchange, converting it into cash and making him and his gang members all rich men. Hughes had a plan, and it involved double-crossing the greedy Estrada.

Hughes said he would accompany Estrada and his men to Monterrey. After the raid, he would then lead them back to the United States to a specific location. Once Estrada's gang and the all of the loot were within the confines of the canyon east of Sloan's Ranch, explained Hughes, Brocious and his gang would ambush them and take the treasure. Hughes's plan appealed to the gang members, and they agreed to send their companion into Sonora to find Estrada.

After weeks of planning and travel, the raid was ready to be launched. Telegraph wires were cut; mules were procured to transport the booty. The bank and church were sacked. During the raid, four Monterrey police officers were shot and killed, along with at least a dozen soldiers. Three hours later, the bandits rode out of town with gold and silver bars and coins, priceless golden statuary from the church, and, to their amazement, a fortune in diamonds that had been stored in the bank's vault—all packed onto their mules.

The outlaws fled due west, following the wagon road to Torreón. Occasional firefights erupted with pursuers, who eventually turned back. Near Torreón, the party turned northward and made their way along a snaking road through the Sierra Madres that eventually took them to an old smuggler's trail that led into Arizona.

Once across the border, the weary bandits made camp in a narrow canyon near the confluence of what is now Skeleton Creek and South Fork Skeleton Creek. By this time, most of Estrada's gang members had been paid off and sent home. The treasure was now guarded by the leader himself, along with a dozen hand-picked men. Hughes told Estrada he was going to ride ahead and make the arrangements for the transfer of the treasure and would return in a few days.

Several days later, Hughes returned to the canyon with Grounds, Hunt, and Neal. For reasons not clear, Brocious remained in Silver City. Early one morning, Hughes led his partners to a point about two miles north of Estrada's camp, where they set up an ambush. At this point, the canyon was so narrow that the mules and riders would have to pass through single file. The Mexicans would be easy targets. When his men were positioned for the assault, Hughes told them to open fire at his signal, which would be a pistol shot. Then he rode back to Estrada's camp.

Hours later, Estrada's men loaded the treasure onto the mules and doused the campfires. The riders mounted and prepared for travel. Hughes told Estrada they were to ride to Silver City, where the treasure would be exchanged for cash. Following the transfer, there would be a celebration. By the time the treasure caravan entered the narrow part of

W. C. JAMESON

the canyon, it was late afternoon. Hughes was in the lead, with Estrada riding behind him.

When the line of riders and pack animals was strung out in the narrow defile, Hughes, riding in the lead, turned in his saddle and shot Estrada in the head. At this, Grounds, Hunt, and Neal opened fire with their rifles, and within seconds, all of the Mexicans were dead.

During the slaughter, the pack mules that were carrying a portion of the treasure panicked and bolted. Unable to overtake and control them, the riders decided that the only way to stop them was to shoot them. All save two were downed before they could escape from the canyon. One was shot just outside of the canyon entrance, and the last was finally overtaken miles away near Geronimo's Peak.

With the killing of the mules, a problem arose. There was no way to transport the greatest portion of the Monterrey loot to the designated hiding place. Neal volunteered to ride to Silver City and secure more mules. Grounds and Hunt would remain in the canyon to guard the treasure. While discussion ensued, Hunt asked why Brocious was to get a share of the treasure when he did nothing to help obtain it. Eventually, it was decided that Hughes would ride back to Silver City and tell Brocious that Estrada had escaped with the treasure. If Brocious acted suspicious, Hughes would kill him. Hughes would then return with the necessary mules; they would load the treasure and transport it to some safe location.

Within hours after Hughes rode away, Grounds, Hunt, and Neal decided to keep the treasure for themselves. With Brocious and Hughes nowhere around, they could divide the fortune three ways. Doc Neal was elected to travel to a nearby ranch and purchase some oxen to carry the treasure. Taking a pocketful of the gold coins, he set out, while Grounds and Hunt set up camp.

Once Neal was out of sight, Grounds and Hunt gathered up the treasure that had been carried by the mules, excavated a deep hole not far from the campsite and about one mile from the massacre site, and buried most of it. According to some estimates, the two men buried, in 1890s values, approximately $80,000 worth of the loot. Some researchers quibble with this figure, claiming it could be as much as one million dollars or more.

Neal rode into camp two days later, leading four oxen roped together. It did not take him long to realize he had been double-crossed by his two partners. He noted that several of the leather pouches containing the treasure lay open and empty, and several of the mule packs were missing. He said nothing, fearing that manifesting his suspicions might get him killed. The following morning, the three men loaded the remaining treasure onto the oxen.

For the next two days, the outlaws herded the oxen northeastward toward New Mexico. Then, just before reaching the border, they turned northward into the Peloncillo Mountains. As they rode along, Neal noted that Grounds and Hunt often rode close together and spoke in whispers. Neal was convinced that the two men intended to kill him. At the first opportunity, he broke away from the pack train and fled eastward. He later reported that Grounds and Hunt fired their rifles at him as he fled, but he was not struck.

Neal rode straight for Silver City. Here, he discovered Brocious had been arrested for fighting and was in the jailhouse. Hughes was living in his cabin. Hughes had not seen Brocious since his return and had been unable to tell him the concocted story of Estrada's escape with the treasure. When Neal told Hughes all that had transpired after he left, Hughes grew angry. The two men decided that when Brocious was released from jail, the three of them would go after Grounds and Hunt.

When Brocious was finally released, Hughes and Neal took him to a saloon, where they explained all that had transpired. Brocious was livid. At some point, a young barmaid banged into his chair and the volatile Brocious, losing control, pulled his revolver and shot her dead. Realizing they were facing serious charges, the three men fled Silver City with a posse on their heels.

Some forty miles later, the posse caught up with the three outlaws at the little town of Shakespeare to the southwest and cornered the outlaws. During the gunfight that ensued, Neal was killed. Brocious and Hughes were forced to surrender and within hours were hanged in the dining room of Shakespeare's Pioneer Hotel.

By the time Brocious and Hughes were dangling from the rafters of the Pioneer, Hunt and Grounds, after filling their pockets with gold coins from the hoard, had buried the remainder of the treasure in a canyon running out of Davis Mountain near Morenci, Arizona. Then, they moved to Tombstone.

Within weeks, word of the massacre of the Estrada gang in what was now being called Skeleton Canyon circulated throughout that part of the

W. C. JAMESON

Southwest; but no one save Grounds and Hunt knew the circumstances. While maintaining their secret, the two men spent their gold recklessly in Tombstone.

Grounds remembered a former girlfriend living in Charleston, a small town not far from Tombstone, and he went to see her. Since Grounds had left, months earlier, she had taken up with the Charleston butcher. When Grounds arrived and showed her all of his gold coins, she decided to go back to him. One night as they were lying together in bed, he told her the story of the Monterrey raid, the treasure, and the incident in Skeleton Canyon. The next morning, after Grounds returned to Tombstone, the woman told the butcher what she had learned. The butcher rode to Tombstone to inform the sheriff, Bill Breckenridge, about the two murderers, Grounds and Hunt, living in his town. While the butcher was talking to Breckenridge, Grounds had returned to Charleston. The girlfriend immediately confessed to him what she had done. Panicked, Grounds rode his horse at a hard gallop back to Tombstone, told Hunt what had happened, and the two fled.

Before leaving, Grounds took a few minutes to write a letter to his mother, who was living in San Antonio, Texas. In the letter, Grounds told her he was coming home, that he was tired of this "wild life." He wrote that he had buried $80,000, which "I came by honestly." He said he intended to purchase a ranch near San Antonio where his mother could live out her days. Enclosed with the letter was a map showing the location of the treasure buried in Skeleton Canyon.

There was no immediate pursuit of Grounds and Hunt, and they spent the night at a ranch owned by a man named Chandler located about ten miles from Tombstone. The next morning, however, the two outlaws were awakened by Sheriff Breckenridge, who called out to them to come out of the bunkhouse with their hands up. Breckenridge, accompanied by two deputies named Gillespie and Young, had followed Grounds and Hunt from Tombstone.

Not wishing to be captured, Grounds and Hunt leaped from the bunk-house, firing their guns. Gillespie was killed immediately, and Young was incapacitated with a bullet in his leg. Breckenridge raised his shotgun and discharged it, the pellets striking Grounds in the head. Dropping the shotgun, the sheriff pulled his revolver and shot Hunt through the chest. The two wounded outlaws were tossed into a buckboard appropriated from rancher Chandler and transported back to Tombstone. Grounds died before arriving, and Hunt was admitted to the local hospital. On first examination, the doctor gave him no chance to live.

Hunt lingered on, requesting authorities contact his brother Hugh. Days later, Hugh arrived from Tucson. The two visited for only a few minutes, then Hugh left. That afternoon, he leased a horse and buggy, clandestinely removed Zwing Hunt from the hospital, and drove out of town. The escape was not discovered until the next day.

On a hunch, Sheriff Breckenridge decided the Hunt brothers were headed to Skeleton Canyon to dig up the treasure. He gathered up a couple of deputies and rode in that direction. Several miles from the massacre site, he encountered a freshly dug grave next to an oak tree. On the trunk of the tree, the name Zwing Hunt was carved. Breckenridge ordered his deputies to dig up the grave. Inside they found Zwing's body. They reburied it and returned to Tombstone. The posse examined the area for a time, but found no evidence of any digging for the treasure.

By now, all of the participants in the caching of the Monterrey loot were dead.

The letter and map that Grounds sent to his mother in San Antonio are still in the possession of his descendants. They are reported to be in good condition, and the map supposedly provides clear directions to the location of the buried treasure. To date, however, no attempt has been made by the Grounds family to recover the buried treasure.

Over the years, many have gone in search of the buried Monterrey loot, popularly known as the Skeleton Canyon Treasure. In Skeleton Canyon, dozens, perhaps hundreds, of gold and silver coins have been found—likely those scattered by the pack mules while attempting to flee the site of the massacre. It has been written that just before he died, Hunt wrote a description of the burial site of the remainder of the treasure that was carried away on the oxen. He stated that it was buried in a canyon near the Davis Mountains. Many consider the directions worthless since there are no Davis Mountains in the area.

It is important to remember, however, that when Grounds and Hunt herded the treasure-laden oxen north after Neal rode away, they traveled for a few more days, turning north near the Arizona–New Mexico border. Conceivably, they could have reached the area of Morenci, Arizona. Just a short distance north of Morenci can be found a Davis Mountain.

The treasure buried in Skeleton Canyon has never been found. If located today, its value could amount to as much as twenty million dollars or more, according to experts. Further, the remainder of the treasure buried in a canyon associated with Davis Mountain near Morenci has never been found, although in 1995 a man exploring in the area encountered evidence of a curious excavation. He also found the remains of oxen buried nearby.

The Lost Iron
Door Mine

During the mid-1700s, the Catholic Church, with the full backing of the government of Spain, operated a rich gold-mining camp in the Santa Catalina Mountains, located a few miles north of Tucson. According to the scant research available, the camp was operated by Jesuits and located near an earlier Spanish mining operation on a mesa in an inaccessible part of the range. As the second camp prospered with the help of Indian slaves, and the community grew in population, a church was built. Legend states that two bells were cast for the church from the gold taken from the mine.

The gold was mined and processed into ingots—thousands of them—until 1767, when the Spanish king Charles III issued an order expelling the Jesuit order from Spain and all its possessions. For months, the Jesuits fought the order, all the while mining the gold in the Santa Catalinas and harvesting even more ore from a placer operation along the Cañada del Oro, a nearby stream. When it became clear that they would soon be evicted by Spanish soldiers, the Jesuits gathered up all of their gold—ingots, nuggets, and dust—and cached it somewhere nearby, presumably in one of the mines. This done, so goes the tale, the entrance was sealed with an iron door. According to a Papago legend handed down in the oral tradition, the immense treasure vault was located somewhere near the south bank of the Cañada del Oro, and the door covered over with rocks to make the site look like the rest of the surroundings.

The Papago slaves who had been forced to work in the mine were freed and returned to their nearby villages. Aside from the handful of priests now fleeing the country, they were the only ones who knew the location of the gold cache and the rich mines.

In June 1789, Apaches attacked the Papago villages in and near the Santa Catalina Mountains, killing most of the residents. For decades, the Apaches ruled the region, and few dared challenge their reign. As late as 1850, a war party of some three hundred Indians raided Tucson and took possession of the town. By 1856, Americans regained the city, but continued to be plagued by Apache raids. Often, the Papagos who lived outside the city sought refuge there from their warring adversaries.

While living in Tucson, an old Papago Indian who had worked in the Jesuits' gold mines related the story of the treasure cache to a number of citizens. He said much gold had been found in and near the Cañada del Oro, a wide, shallow, southward-running stream found along the western base of the mountains. East of the lower end of the canyon, he said, was a low mesa upon which there could be found the ruins of the old Jesuit camp. One listener calculated that if the Indian was correct, the gold would lie only seventeen miles from the middle of downtown Tucson.

During the first decade of the twentieth century, an elderly man opened a small grocery store on North Sixth Avenue in Tucson. As he cleaned the building prior to moving in, he discovered a sheet of parchment in an old, abandoned wooden trunk. The parchment contained written directions to what was called the Escalante Mine. According to the document, the mine was located approximately one league northwest of a natural landform called La Ventana—"The Window." La Ventana was a natural rectangular hole in the rock in the Santa Catalina Mountains. The document further stated that when the miners stood at the entrance to the shaft, they could look toward the southeast and through La Ventana.

A Papago who worked as a cowhand for several area ranchers claimed he knew where the window was located. He also said he had found one of the gold mines. He related that while riding his pony in the Santa Catalinas on a particularly windy day, he heard a low moaning sound he thought was coming from a dense clump of brush several dozen yards off the trail. Deciding to investigate, the cowhand walked through the brush and, on the other side in the wall of the canyon, discovered the wind was blowing across a small hole and making the eerie noise. He realized at once it was the entrance to a mine shaft.

Bending low, the cowhand entered the shaft, and within a few yards encountered small piles of gold ore. It appeared, he said, as if the gold were waiting to be smelted, or transported to some location to be processed. Although the cowhand spoke of his find to other Indians and to his Mexican friends, he refused to lead anyone to the location.

In researching the mining of gold in the areas of the Santa Catalinas, an account of a gold discovery in 1843 was encountered. On June 29 of that year, Colonel Antonio P. Narbona led a military detachment into the Santa Catalina Mountains in search of Apaches. His orders were to drive the Indians from the range, killing or capturing as many as possible.

Just before sundown, Narbona led his men into the Cañada del Oro and to a water hole several hundred yards from the lower reaches. With good water and some graze for the horses, he ordered camp to be set up. That night, after dining, several of the soldiers walked over to the tiny creek that ran from the spring to wash dishes. As they rinsed the plates and cutlery, they spied small flakes of gold on the stream bottom. They were not permitted to pan the gold, however, for the mission was to chase Apaches.

In 1858, a small party of prospectors made camp at the same location and spent several weeks panning gold from the stream. Repeated raids by Apaches, however, forced them to leave the area and never return. By 1870, the location of the placer gold in the Cañada del Oro was known to many in Tucson, and weekends found a dozen or more at the site sifting gold from the bottom sands. One afternoon, Apaches swooped down on the miners, killing them all, and it was years before anyone entered the region again.

In 1880, Solomon M. Allis was camped in the northwestern end of the Santa Catalinas. Allis was a surveyor and part-time prospector. Years later, he would be named United States deputy mineral surveyor. One night, as he sat next to his campfire, he was visited by two prospectors who related an amazing tale: they claimed they had found a gold mine that was sealed with an iron door.

According to the story told by the men, they had been prospecting in the Mexican state of Sonora the previous year when they stopped to request water from a well near a remote adobe dwelling several miles from the town of Caborca. The old man and woman who lived there invited the prospectors to spend the night and share their dinner with them. During conversation, it was learned that the men were from Arizona, and the host, who said he was a Papago, asked them if they had ever heard of the mine with the iron door. When they admitted they had

W. C. JAMESON

not, the old man produced a diary once owned by his grandfather. His grandfather, he said, had been forced to work in the mine by the Jesuits, and was one of the men who had assisted in installing the iron door.

The two prospectors studied the diary and found numerous entries testifying to the harvesting of two hundred or more pounds of almost pure gold in a day! They encountered another entry detailing directions to the mine and copied it. Several days later, they made preparations to depart for Arizona and the Santa Catalina Mountains.

On January 10, 1881, the two men found themselves at the south entrance to the Cañada del Oro. After riding a short distance into the canyon, they dismounted, hobbled their horses and burros, and proceeded on foot up what they identified as a middle canyon. It was very rugged and narrow. That night they set up camp near a small spring. The next morning, they hiked and climbed another five miles, reaching a point where the canyon divided. Following the directions they had copied from the old Papago diary, they turned right. Within one half mile they arrived at a cul-de-sac, steep walls on all sides.

After an hour of examining the cul-de-sac, one of the prospectors found some very old and eroded hand-carved steps in the left-hand wall. Leaving their packs behind, and with great caution, they climbed the steps and found themselves on a rock ledge several dozen feet above the floor of the canyon. Here, they found a cave. One of the prospectors returned to his pack and retrieved two candles. Lighting them, the men entered the cave. After following the passageway for several yards, they were about to conclude that it amounted to little more than a part-time habitation for ancient Indians. Then, one of the men spotted an inscription in one wall. *Dominus vobiscum*, the Latin blessing, had been painstakingly chiseled into the rock. Seeing the inscription as a sign, they continued on, eventually discerning light ahead. Presently, they came to the end of the cave—which opened out onto the face of a sheer cliff overlooking a valley.

Determining there was no safe descent, the second prospector made his way back through the cave, down the steps, and to the packs. From these, he retrieved several lengths of rope. Returning to the far outlet of the cave, the men tied the ropes together and descended two hundred feet to the floor of the valley below. Here they found a narrow stream with fish. They caught several for dinner, and while cleaning them, they spotted nuggets of gold on the creek's sandy bottom. They managed to harvest a few nuggets before sunset. The two made a rude camp on the bank of the stream, and in the morning proceeded eastward up the valley. Before long, they arrived on top of a mesa and came to the ruins of a small, long-abandoned settlement. One of the buildings resembled a church. Several of the stones in the church bore Latin inscriptions.

The two men spent the next three days searching for the mine—the one with the iron door. On the third day they found it. The door, along with the bars that secured it, had succumbed to heavy rusting. The fittings had broken loose, and the door lay on the ground in front of an opening. Ten minutes after entering the shaft, the prospectors found a ten-to-twelve-inch-wide vein of quartz laced throughout with gold. The vein stretched four hundred feet into the mine. On the floor of the shaft were a number of tools that had apparently been dropped after the miners employed them for the final time.

For several days, the two prospectors hacked gold from the vein of quartz, filling a number of ore sacks with the mineral. When they had harvested all they could carry, they left and made their way back down the valley, made the difficult climb up the face of the cliff to the cave, went through it, and came back out into the canyon. Before leaving the mine, they erected location notices. On leaving the canyon, their first order of business was to register their discovery. They were on their way to Oracle to do so when they encountered Allis, the surveyor, in his camp. When Allis admitted that the story possessed elements of the fantastic, the two prospectors emptied their packs and showed him approximately one hundred pounds of gold they had managed to carry out of the mine.

Allis offered to finance the return trip to the Lost Iron Door Mine. The two prospectors agreed, and together the three settled on an arrangement. Allis remained in his camp while the two men went to Oracle to file their claim. Days passed, and the prospectors did not return. Curious, Allis traveled to Oracle to find out what he could of the two men. Two days after arriving, he learned that they had been killed in an accident. During his discussion with the two prospectors, Allis had never thought to inquire about specific directions to the Lost Iron Door Mine.

Allis told the story of meeting the two prospectors, and of their adventure and discovery of the Lost Iron Door Mine. Since then, dozens of hardy adventurers have entered the realm of the Santa Catalina Mountains and the Cañada del Oro in search of the Lost Iron Door Mine. None were successful.

W. C. JAMESON

In 1991, a backpacker was exploring a portion of the Santa Catalina Mountains. He had become lost, and after two days of hiking found himself atop a low mesa. As he searched for a way down other than the trail he had come up, he encountered the ruin of an old settlement. One of the tumbled-down buildings, he said, looked like it might have been a church. In fact, he claimed, several of the stones that made up the wall of the building had Latin inscriptions on them. The backpacker wandered around for two days searching for a route to safety. On the evening of the second day, he made a small camp near a *tinaja* that had captured a significant amount of water from a rain the week before. As he lay in his sleeping bag, he watched as a swarm of bats exited an opening in the nearby cliff face. The next morning, he walked over to the hole and discovered it to be an ancient mine shaft. Oddly, lying in front of the entrance was a rusted iron door. Since he had a fear of closed-in spaces, and since several rattlesnakes had taken shade just inside the entrance, he declined to enter.

Three days later he made it to civilization. He was weak and dehydrated, and after several days of rest and rehydration, he returned to his home in Texas. Years later, he learned the story of the Lost Iron Door Mine and realized that during his plight in the Santa Catalina Mountains, he had encountered it by accident. He realized he had been only a few yards away from millions of dollars worth of gold. During a subsequent trip to the range, he searched for the lost mine, but never found it.

To date, hundreds have entered the Santa Catalina Mountains in search of the Lost Iron Door Mine, all in hopes of finding the gold and growing wealthy in the blink of an eye. Several have invested thousands of dollars in the venture, and at least four people have entered the range and never come out.

The Lost Iron Door Mine, with the great treasure cache of the Jesuits, still resides in the Santa Catalina Mountains, still tempting those not immune to the lure of treasure.

Silver
Mountain

During skirmishes with Apaches in east-central Arizona during the mid-1800s, white settlers were startled to discover that the Indians were using silver instead of lead to manufacture bullets for their rifles. This was first noticed when a wagon train traveling from Missouri to Southern California was attacked near Carrizo Creek in eastern Arizona. No one was killed, but when the Apaches retreated, the wagon-train scout dug two silver bullets out of a saddle that had been hit. Several of the members of the wagon-train party wanted to remain in the area and try to learn the source of the silver, but the hostile nature of the indigenes precluded a lengthy stay.

During the 1860s, a young Mexican named Juan Encinas was captured by a band of Apaches near Tucson. Encinas was taken northeast to an Indian stronghold near the headwaters of the White River and used as a slave. The headwaters are near the present-day town of Eagar. During his seven years of captivity, Encinas was put to work digging silver ore from a remote mine. The silver was nearly pure, with only small percentages of lead and zinc. The Apaches used the ore for making bullets.

One morning, Encinas escaped while most of the fighting men were out on a raid. Barefooted and with no food or water, he walked southward into the desert, where he was found by a small group of Mexican miners close to the Sonoran border. Hungry and exhausted, Encinas was taken in and cared for by the miners. Following a week of recovery, Encinas told the miners of his years as a slave to the Apaches. He related how he was made to walk a long distance to a location at what the Indians called Silver Mountain. There, he was forced to dig the ore from a thick vein that extended well over one hundred yards across a rock outcrop and deep into the mountain. In addition, he said, large chunks of silver that had weathered from the vein lay scattered across the ground, making it difficult to walk. Impressed with the story, the miners persuaded Encinas to lead them to Silver Mountain.

Two weeks later, the party headed north, entering Apache country. They were spotted and trailed, the Indians waiting for an opportunity to attack. Because the miners were poorly armed and fearful of the menacing Apaches, they decided to return to Mexico.

In 1890, Pedro Encinas, a nephew of Juan, led another party of miners into Apache country for the express purpose of locating the silver mine. Pedro carried a map he claimed was made by his uncle and which purported to show the exact location of the ore. Encinas refused to show the map to anyone.

While traveling through the San Carlos Indian Reservation in southwestern Arizona, he was visited in camp by W. J. Ellis, the agent in charge. When Ellis asked Encinas what business he had on the reservation, the Mexican explained that he was searching for a silver mine. Following a pleasant conversation, Ellis granted Encinas permission to hunt for the mine, but told him that he would not be allowed to remove any of the ore from government-controlled land. Encinas agreed, and for several weeks searched throughout the region.

Then, one day he and his men found the mine. It was exactly as his uncle had described it—fist-sized silver nuggets lying about the ground, and an impressive vein of ore that could be seen snaking along a granite outcrop for dozens of yards. Encinas and his men gathered up four pouchfuls of the ore, returned to reservation headquarters, and presented them to agent Ellis. Encinas explained to Ellis that he would abide by the agreement not to take any of the silver from the reservation, but told Ellis that if the government ever changed its policy, he would like to be contacted. Ellis assured him he would.

Encinas bid Ellis good day and was preparing to leave when the agent asked him for directions to the mine. Politely, Encinas explained to Ellis that until permission to extract the silver was formally granted by the government, the location would remain a secret. He assured the agent that when such permission was granted, that he, Ellis, would be considered for a share, and the location would be revealed. With that, Encinas gathered up the members of his party and departed, presumably to Mexico.

Several years later, the San Carlos Reservation was temporarily opened up to prospectors. Agent Ellis, however, was no longer living, and Pedro Encinas was never informed. In fact, when Encinas returned to Mexico, he was never heard from again.

In 1940, a man named L. K. Thompson, a resident of the tiny community of Salt River, was interviewed by a newspaper reporter interested in his experiences as a young man living in the wild and unsettled days of early Arizona. It was discovered during the interview that Thompson was a brother-in-law to Pedro Encinas and had accompanied him on the 1890 expedition to find Silver Mountain.

Thompson explained that Silver Mountain was never located within the boundaries of the San Carlos Indian Reservation. He said that it was, in fact, located just inside the boundary of the old White Mountain Indian Reservation. Thompson stated that Encinas never trusted agent Ellis and deceived him about the location. Thompson went on to explain that while Encinas made it appear that he was camped on the San Carlos Reservation, he was, in truth, digging the silver from the vein located on Silver Mountain. Over the years, Encinas returned to Silver Mountain several times. Following each visit, he hauled several wagonloads of the ore back to Mexico, where it was sold. In time, Pedro Encinas became a rich man.

When Thompson was asked why he never returned to the mountain to dig some of the silver for himself, he explained that he believed the site was cursed. Several of the miners had died there, he said, all from unexplainable accidents. He stayed with Encinas for one year and decided it was not worth the risk.

According to Thompson, Silver Mountain, a name known only to the Apaches, is in a remote area and seldom visited. The nuggets, he said, are still lying about on the ground, and the thick, rich vein still gleams brightly in the morning sun.

W. C. JAMESON

Spanish Padres' Lost Gold Cache

In response to the growing settlements near the mineral-rich mountains around Tubac, a man named Hardwick, believing he could make money providing supplies to the area miners and ranchers, established a mercantile during the late 1870s. In a short time, Hardwick realized that the customers who frequented his store had very little money and grudgingly shelled out a few coins or an occasional small poke of gold dust now and then for coffee, beans, flour, and sugar. Hardwick considered closing his store and trying his luck in the goldfields himself, when a significant event occurred.

Among Hardwick's customers were a few Indians who lived in the area, mostly Papagos. One occasional visitor to the store was an elderly Papago who always paid for his goods with gold nuggets. His purchases were modest, and he carried them to his small rock and adobe home, where he lived with his wife. Hardwick maintained a curiosity about the old Indian. He considered him far too old and feeble to be involved in the hard work of mining gold.

On one occasion, the old man came to the store in need of a few goods and explained to Hardwick that he had no gold with him, but would retrieve some in the near future and bring it to him. The storekeeper had no reason to distrust the old Indian and thus extended him credit. Two weeks later, the Papago arrived at the store and paid off the merchant.

Hardwick was aware that, other than for trade and perhaps ornaments, the Indians had little use for gold. It was even odder to encounter an Indian who mined his own. Unable to contain his curiosity, Hardwick was determined to find out more. The next time the Indian came in to purchase foodstuffs, the storekeeper asked him in what range of mountains was his gold mine. The Indian replied only that it was hidden.

A few years passed, and the old Indian became more and more feeble. He could barely walk, and his trips to the mercantile became fewer. On one occasion, he arrived at the store, selected a few goods, and piled them on the counter. When Hardwick added them up and told the Papago the price, the Indian withdrew a gold ingot one foot long and an inch and a half wide. Hardwick's eyes bulged at the sight of the bar. He weighed it and told the Papago that this single ingot would pay for all of his goods for the next two years.

The Indian explained to Hardwick that in recent weeks he had grown so weak with age that he was unable to reach the large cache of gold nuggets he normally used to pay for his food. He explained that the gold ingot was one of hundreds that were stacked closer to the entrance of the cave where they were stored. Hardwick walked to the front of the store, locked the door, and invited the old man to the storeroom in the back. After offering him a seat, Hardwick confessed his curiosity over the source of the gold the Indian brought to the mercantile.

The old man thought for a while and then told Hardwick that he would tell him the story of the gold. He told him that he was growing old and the trip to town was becoming difficult. He further explained that his wife was ill and would not live much longer either. And then he told Hardwick an amazing story.

Years ago, explained the old man, back in the time of his own grandfather, the Jesuits who lived in the mission had accumulated a great deal of gold and silver from mines they oversaw in the region. The ore was dug from the mines by Indians who were enslaved for the task. The Papago's own grandfather had lost relatives to the difficult work in the mines. They were chained neck to neck and forced to work from dawn to past dark on meager rations. Many died in their chains.

Some of the gold and silver was melted down and formed into ingots. The nuggets that were not melted were stored in leather bags. As the years passed, enough gold and silver was accumulated to fill a large room in the mission.

A day came when the Jesuits received word from their superiors in Spain that they were being called back, and that the mission was to be abandoned. The Jesuits had all of the gold and silver loaded onto burros and carried away to a secret location, where it was hidden. It was a

W. C. JAMESON

cave, explained the old Indian, and the entrance was located in a seldom-traveled valley in an unnamed range of mountains not far from the mission. The Jesuits covered the entrance to make it look like the rest of the mountain.

Years passed. When the Papago was a young man, he took a wife. In searching for a place to live where he could raise a few goats and grow some corn, he found a quiet valley in a range of mountains not far from the mission. Here, a small stream ran year-round and the soil was fertile. He and his wife labored for weeks on the construction of a small house. Life was good for the Indian and his mate.

One day, said the Papago, his wife was cooking the evening meal on a small fire in an outdoor pit in front of the house. It was dusk, and following a long day of laboring in his garden, the Indian leaned back against a willow rack and watched the smoke from the fire curl skyward. As his eyes followed the spiraling smoke, he was distracted by what he perceived as a large dark cloud forming near the ridge of the adjacent mountain. Odd, he thought—for the day had been clear, with no suggestion of approaching rain.

As he observed the cloud, it began moving rapidly down the slope of the mountain and then dispersed. Suddenly, the Indian realized it was a great flight of bats undertaking their nocturnal feeding on insects. For several evenings in a row, the young man watched the bats and determined the location of their exit from the mountain. It was a narrow, barely perceptible opening high on the side, almost to the top. The cavern from which they came must be immense, thought the Indian, to house so many millions of bats.

Weeks later, when he had completed his work early, the Papago climbed the side of the low mountain to inspect the opening. He came to a long, thin cleft. The opening was taller than he, but so narrow he had to turn sideways to enter. He passed through and went several paces into the cave until it became too dark to see. The cave, he could tell, continued on for a great distance. He determined that at the first opportunity he would carry torches up to the cave and explore.

More time passed, and one day when he finished his chores early, the Papago fashioned several torches from reeds that grew along the stream bank. He carried them up the steep slope to the opening and passed within. Lighting one of the torches, he proceeded along the narrow, twisting passage.

For many yards the passageway continued, widening as it proceeded deeper and lower into the mountain. Soon, the Indian came to a large room wide enough to accommodate his herd of thirty goats and high enough that a man standing on the shoulders of another would barely reach the ceiling. From this room, two additional passageways were evident. The Indian selected one and entered.

He realized at once that it was no longer entirely a natural cavern he now explored, but a man-made tunnel. Every few paces, heavy timbers shored up the passageway. After several minutes, the Indian arrived at a dead end. On examination, it appeared that he had reached the entrance of the mine, but that it had been filled with rock and debris, effectively sealing it off from the outside. He returned to the large room and entered the other passageway.

This route was also a man-made shaft shored up with timbers like the previous one. As he proceeded through the tunnel, the Papago noted that it gradually widened, eventually opening up into a room not as large as the previous one. Here, he found benches and a table, such as one would associate with a church. It would appear, he considered, as though services were held in this place.

The light from the Papago's torch reflected from an object against the far wall. On investigation, he discovered it was a statue of one of the saints and made from solid gold. Nearby he found several more golden statues of other saints and the Virgin Mary. Lying on the ground was a golden crucifix. Beyond this room was another tunnel, lower and narrower than the rest. Stooping, the Indian entered it, lighting another torch as he went. Several paces into the tunnel he found gold and silver bars stacked against one wall. He estimated there were thousands of them. At the end of the stacks were dozens of leather sacks, each filled with gold nuggets and dust. Beyond these, he found several skeletons. Each had an iron collar around the neck, and all were linked by long-rusted chains.

As the Indian stood in awe, staring at the skeletons and the immense wealth of gold and silver, he realized he had stumbled upon the long-lost treasure of the Tubac mission padres.

He noted he was down to one torch and that it would be just enough to get him back to the narrow entrance high on the side of the mountain if he hurried. Making his way through the tunnels and the large room, he noted even more sacks piled in the dark corners. He assumed these also

W. C. JAMESON

contained gold and silver. On subsequent explorations into the mine, that proved to be correct.

On exiting the underground chamber at the narrow cleft, the Indian sat on the ground in front of the opening and pondered what to do about this newfound wealth. Like many Indians, as well as Mexicans, the Papago believed such treasure was invariably associated with spirits, not all of them good ones. It was believed by many that to retrieve wealth that was lost or hidden was to invite bad luck. He thought about this for an hour and finally decided to leave it where it lay. He made his way down the mountainside and returned to his home and wife. Months passed before he said anything to her about the great treasure he had found in the cave.

More time passed, and the Papago and his wife grew old. No longer did they have a goat herd, for predation by wolves and mountain lions had taken their number. Years of drought had caused the creek to dry up, and what they were able to coax from their poor garden was dependent on the occasional rainfall that visited that arid part of the Southwest. Sometimes days would pass when the two old Indians had nothing to eat.

In desperation, the old Papago decided to avail himself of some of the gold hidden in the adjacent mountain. With great difficulty, he climbed the mountain, entered the narrow cleft, and walked the passageways to the bags of gold nuggets. He filled his pockets and made his way out of the chamber and down the mountain. It was around that time that he began visiting the mercantile near Tubac and trading with Hardwick. In time, the Papago learned to carry extra bags of nuggets, as well as gold ingots, back to his secret entrance and stack them there so he would not have to traverse the entire cavern with each trip.

The old Indian explained to Hardwick that he felt bad about taking the gold, and that he prayed every day that no harm would befall him or his wife. Hardwick, in turn, assured the Papago that such things were superstitions and nothing would ever come of it. The storekeeper also invested a great deal of time and energy in convincing the Indian that he should reveal the location of the mine to someone he trusted, and suggested himself.

At first, the Papago demurred. He admitted to Hardwick that, besides his wife of many years, the storekeeper was the only person he ever had any contact with, and that it likely would hurt nothing to tell him. As the Papago provided directions, Hardwick wrote them down:

Travel to the third low mountain to the southwest. Wait at the foot of the mountain until evening when you will see a great cloud of bats rising above the rim. At the point where they exit the mountain is an entrance to the cave where the Spanish padres stored their treasure.

With head bowed, the Papago bade Hardwick good day and left.

Hardwick was so obsessed with the notion that within hours he would be wealthy that he could not sleep that night. The following morning he did not open his store. Instead, he gathered a number of burlap sacks that he intended to fill with treasure and departed for the third low mountain to the southwest. Weary, he arrived at the location just as the sun was beginning to set. In his haste, Hardwick had forgotten to pack food, so he was also hungry. He built a small fire for warmth, and leaned back against a log to watch for the bats so he could determine the location on the mountain from which they came. With fatigue overtaking Hardwick and the warmth of the fire offering comfort, the storekeeper soon fell asleep.

Later, he awoke with a start. It was dark, and here and there he spotted bats flitting around in the dark in search of insects. He realized that he had missed the bats exiting the cavern. Discouraged, he returned to his store, determined to try again after making better preparations.

Two days later, the Papago arrived at the mercantile. He asked Hardwick if he had found the entrance to the cave. The storekeeper explained to the Indian that he had fallen asleep and missed the opportunity, but would try again in the next day or two.

The Indian breathed a sigh of relief and told Hardwick it was good he had not located the opening. He confessed that after revealing the location of the entrance to the treasure cave, he began to have bad feelings, that he had done something wrong, and that he might have jeopardized the storekeeper's life. He said that no good would come from removing the lost treasure of the Spanish padres from its hiding place. Then he told Hardwick that he had climbed to the entrance and filled it with rocks and sticks and brush so that the bats could not come out. He explained to Hardwick that no bats would ever come from the cave again, and that he had been wrong to reveal the secret location. The secret, he explained, was not his to reveal.

W. C. JAMESON

Most researchers who have studied this tale are convinced that the third low mountain to the southwest of Tubac is located in the Baboquivari Mountain Range near the small town of Arivaca in Pima County. That this area has been a source of gold was never in doubt, for during the late 1800s, small fortunes were taken from placer mines along the small creeks in the range.

Burt Alvord's
Gold

Burt Alvord was one of several colorful characters who frequented southeastern Arizona during the late 1800s. And like many outlaws of his day, he spent some time as a lawman. He was good at both professions, but he once claimed that being an outlaw was more exciting than being a peace officer.

Alvord's origins are vague. What is known, however, is that as a youth he worked at the OK Corral in Tombstone, mucking out stables and running errands. He claimed he watched the famous shootout between the Earp brothers and the Clantons. When he was nineteen, Alvord shot and killed his first man in a gunfight on the streets of Tombstone.

A few months after he turned twenty, Alvord was hired as a deputy by Cochise County sheriff John Slaughter. Slaughter often had high praise for Alvord, and the two men were regarded as an effective law-enforcement team for four years. So much so, in fact, that at the end of his term, Sheriff Slaughter declared Cochise County rid of all bad men and ne'er-do-wells and retired. Alvord was encouraged to run for the office, but declared he had had enough of law enforcement and sought other adventures.

A short time later, Alvord traveled to the Mexican state of Sonora. Before long, he discovered that rustling cattle was easy and profitable. Alvord's successful raids on the area cattle ranches generated attention from police, and after several months they were closing in on him and his operation. Before he could be apprehended, he decided to leave Mexico. He returned to Tombstone in search of work. Citizens there still remembered him as a competent lawman, and before too much time passed, he took a job as constable of the small community of Fairbanks, located five miles northwest of Tombstone. A few weeks later, he went to work as a constable in Willcox, a growing mining town in the northern part of Cochise County.

While in Willcox, Alvord became acquainted with Billy Stiles, who was a policeman in the small town of Pearce, some thirty miles due south. Stiles had a reputation of being a bully, and a bit too quick and eager to use his gun. It was rumored that he shot and killed his own father when he was twelve years old. Regardless, Alvord saw something in Stiles he liked and hired him as a deputy.

Alvord, Stiles, and another Willcox deputy named Robert Downing decided that crime paid more than law enforcement, and they began planning their first robbery.

They learned that within the week, a Southern Pacific train carrying a Wells Fargo shipment of $60,000 in gold coins and bullion would stop briefly at the station in Cochise, a tiny community ten miles southwest of Willcox. While preparations for the robbery were being made, the three met an out-of-work cowhand named Burt Matts and invited him to join them.

Late evening on September 9, 1899, the Southern Pacific westbound train stopped at the station in Cochise. As the train took on water, Stiles and Matts, with revolvers drawn and masks over their faces, climbed into the engine cab. Stiles shoved his handgun into the face of the engineer and ordered him to uncouple the engine and express car from the rest of the train. Once this was done, they instructed the engineer to move a mile up the track.

At a selected spot west of Cochise, the train stopped. Nearby were staked out two saddled horses as well as two pack horses. Stiles and Matts tied up the engineer and, leaving him in the cab, proceeded toward the express car. Knowing that the car would be locked, they had brought dynamite. After setting the charge, they blew the door away, sending it crashing to the ground. When they scrambled into the express car, they encountered a guard who had been knocked unconscious by the blast. A moment later, they found several heavy bags containing the gold. With difficulty, they pulled the bags from the car, loaded them into their saddlebags and packs on two additional horses, and fled into the night.

As planned, the two outlaws rode to an abandoned cabin set a few hundred feet off the Cochise–Willcox road. When they rode up to the cabin, Alvord was waiting for them. After dismounting, the bandits were given a change of clothes by Alvord. As they dressed, Alvord counted out $350 for each of them as well as for Downing, who remained in Willcox. This done, he told Stiles and Matts to remain in the cabin while he buried the loot nearby. Alvord led the gold-laden horses one hundred yards away, excavated a shallow hole, and placed the gold within. After covering it, he returned to the cabin. He explained that when the excitement of the robbery had died down in a few weeks, they would return to this place, dig up the gold, and divide it equally. He cautioned Downing, Matts, and Stiles to be careful about how they spent their $350. The last thing they needed was to attract attention. The outlaws then split up, each taking a different route back to town.

Alvord arrived in Willcox at dawn and rode directly to his office. He had no sooner got a pot of coffee boiling when a messenger arrived from Cochise informing him that the Southern Pacific train had been held up and the Wells Fargo gold shipment taken by two masked outlaws. Knowing this would happen, Alvord summoned several men to serve as a posse. He divided them into three groups. He placed himself in charge of one and Stiles and Downing each in charge of the other two. For two days, the three lawmen/bandits led the posses in circles, eventually returning to Willcox. Alvord reported to Wells Fargo that no sign of the train robbers could be found.

Days later, a Wells Fargo agent named John Thacker arrived in Willcox. He introduced himself to Alvord and Stiles and told them he would be investigating the train robbery. Alvord told Thacker that his office was prepared to cooperate in the matter. Alvord was convinced that Thacker would soon grow discouraged at not finding any evidence of the train robbers and leave. Just as it seemed that would be the case, Robert Downing made a grave mistake.

During the evening before Thacker was to leave Willcox, Downing sat down to play cards at a local tavern and started drinking heavily. After an hour, Downing was losing big. He was about to quit the game when he remembered he had some of the coins from the train robbery in his pockets. He withdrew a number of the newly minted ten-dollar gold pieces and continued playing. Word of Downing's newfound wealth soon reached Thacker, and the agent paid a visit to the tavern.

Unknown to Downing, Thacker observed the game. He spotted the gold pieces and recognized them as part of the Wells Fargo shipment that had been stolen. Thacker considered arresting Downing, then remembered that the gambler was wellconnected to the two lawmen, Alvord and Stiles. Thacker decided to remain in town for a while in hopes that the bandits would trip themselves up.

Unaware of Thacker's discovery, Alvord and Stiles began making plans for another train robbery. For this job, they enlisted the help of several local men they had come to trust: Bob Brown, Bravo Juan Yoas, brothers George and Louis Owens, and "Three-Fingered Jack" Dunlop. For reasons unknown, Alvord and Stiles elected not to include Downing and Matts.

Alvord received information that an express train carrying another Wells Fargo gold shipment would stop for the night at Fairbanks. Having been the Fairbanks constable, Alvord knew the town well, and explained to his companions that only a few people lived there and pursuit would be negligible to nonexistent.

Alvord also learned that the express-car guard was a man named Jeff Milton, and he began to grow concerned. Milton was a former Texas Ranger and was reputed to be tough as nails and a crack shot.

Milton was riding in the express car on the night of February 15, 1900, when the train pulled to a stop at Fairbanks. As the train took on water, he slid open the heavy door to get some fresh air. As he stood in the opening, smoking a cigarette, he heard someone order him to raise his hands. Thinking it was a prank, Milton ignored the command and continued to smoke. A second later, a gunshot erupted out of the night, the bullet striking the door next to which he stood. A second later another shot rang out, and Milton was struck in the arm and knocked to the floor of the car.

Three-Fingered Jack Dunlop and Bravo Juan Yoas, believing Milton dead, climbed into the express car. In the darkness, Milton had crawled over to his sawed-off shotgun and awaited his attackers. As the silhouettes of the two would-be robbers appeared in the doorway, Milton pulled the trigger. Dunlop, his chest filled with buckshot, toppled from the doorway to the ground. Yoas, having been struck by a single pellet, uttered a cry of pain, leaped to the ground, mounted his horse, and rode away.

The Owens brothers and Brown, who were standing just outside the express-car door, opened fire with their rifles, hoping to kill whoever was inside. Milton, in pain and bleeding from his wound, pulled the keys to the safe from his shirt pocket and tossed them behind some baggage.

After reloading his shotgun, he sat back and readied himself for the second wave of bandits to enter the car. A moment later, he passed out.

Alvord leaped into the boxcar and assessed the situation. Believing Milton dead, he searched his pockets for the keys to the Wells Fargo safe. When he could not find them, he cursed. Counting on having access to the keys, Alvord had decided not to bring dynamite. Frustrated, he left the express car. After hoisting the severely wounded Dunlop onto his saddle, the outlaws dashed away. After five minutes on the trail, Dunlop proved to be a problem. He kept falling from his saddle, so the outlaws decided to abandon him and continue on their flight.

This proved to be an error in judgment. The following morning, a posse found Dunlop on the side of the road. Mortally wounded, he lay under some low-growing brush nine miles from the railroad tracks. When one of the deputies told Dunlop that his wounds were fatal and he would die within hours, the outlaw decided to take revenge on those who had abandoned him. Gasping for breath, and with blood leaking from his mouth, Dunlop named Alvord, Stiles, the Owens brothers, and Bob Brown as the men who attempted to rob the express car.

The following morning, Alvord and Stiles were arrested and placed in the Cochise County jail. Stiles was promised a light sentence if he would testify against Alvord and reveal where the Wells Fargo gold stolen in September 1899 was hidden. Stiles explained to his interrogators that Alvord had hidden the gold and the location was known only to him. He agreed to testify against his companion and was released on bond. While free, Stiles broke Alvord out of jail on April 10, 1900, and the two fled to Mexico, where they were convinced they would be safe from pursuit.

Wells Fargo authorities determined that flight to Mexico should not guarantee safety to the two bandits. They hired two former Texas Rangers to cross the border and track down the pair. In February 1904, the Rangers came upon Alvord and Stiles in their hideout deep in Sonora. When the two outlaws refused to surrender, a gunfight broke out. Alvord was severely wounded and surrendered. Stiles held the Rangers off until dark, then mounted up and rode away. After treating Alvord's wounds, the two Rangers loaded him onto a horse and transported him back to Arizona to stand trial.

Alvord was found guilty of train robbery and sentenced to ten years in the Yuma Territorial Prison. After sentencing, Wells Fargo representatives tried to make a deal with the outlaw. If he would tell them where

W. C. JAMESON

the gold from the Southern Pacific train robbery was hidden, they promised they would intercede for him and get his sentence reduced. Alvord told them to go to hell.

As it turned out, Alvord served only two years of his sentence. It is believed by some that Wells Fargo authorities arranged for the early release so they could follow the bandit to where he had hidden the gold. From the moment he left the prison at Yuma, Alvord was tailed by Wells Fargo agents wherever he went. He made several attempts to lose them, but was never successful. He decided not to lead them to the gold cache located near the Cochise–Willcox road. Frustrated, Alvord decided to leave the country. He traveled to California and then booked passage to Panama. Within his first few weeks in Latin America, he was introduced to the widow of a multimillionaire. In time, they married. Alvord lived out the rest of his life in the Canal Zone and died a wealthy man.

After Billy Stiles escaped, it was reported that he traveled in Mexico for a while and then went to China. After several years, he returned to the United States, assumed the alias of William Larkin, and secured a job as a deputy sheriff in Nevada. The former train robber died in 1908, shot by a twelve-year-old boy, the son of a man Stiles had killed weeks earlier.

Neither Alvord nor Stiles were ever able to return to the lonely cabin on the old Cochise–Willcox road to retrieve the buried gold. It is presumed that the hoard still remains under a few inches of Arizona sand. If found today, the cache would be worth in the neighborhood of one-third of a million dollars.

No one is certain of the exact location of the old abandoned cabin where Alvord met Stiles and Matts after they robbed the train. It is likely that the structure has weathered and collapsed in the more than a century that had passed since the robbery. Still, some part of the old habitation must exist, and if found, would serve as the key to the location of the buried Wells Fargo gold.

Lost Arroyo
Gold

The U.S. Army cavalry troop had been in pursuit of the renegade Apaches for several days. Despite hard riding with little rest, they were no closer to them than when they started. The band of Indians, estimated to be fifteen, had fled the reservation one week earlier. The latest intelligence had the band making a wide detour around Phoenix and heading toward a well-known campsite on the banks of the Gila River, a place called Maricopa Well. The year was 1870, and tensions between the Apaches and the military were high.

When the troopers rode up on Maricopa Well, their hearts sank. They saw smoke rising from a still-smoldering ox-drawn wagon. Evidence suggested that a family on their way west had stopped to camp for the night and were surprised by the Apaches. The oxen had been cut loose and herded away. A man, his wife, and two small children lay dead and scalped next to the looted wagon. Following an investigation at the site, it was learned there had been another child, an older girl. The lieutenant in charge concluded that she had been taken captive by the Apaches.

Two of the scouts informed the lieutenant that the tracks of the Indians led south toward Mexico. A scout was dispatched to Fort Tucson to report the attack and the probable route taken by the escaping Apaches. On receiving the report, the post commander sent a mounted company of troopers under the command of a Captain Erickson to try to intercept the murderers and rescue the girl.

Erickson double-timed the company of cavalry westward in hopes of overtaking the Indians before they crossed into Mexico. Days later, they found themselves in a vast waterless tract of the Sonoran desert. All of their canteens and water barrels were empty, and men and horses alike were suffering from thirst. Late one afternoon, an Indian scout rode in from the point and informed Erickson that his horse was behaving as if it had scented water. He asked for permission to allow his mount to lead them to the source. Erickson assented, and the column of riders turned northwestward toward a depression in the landscape several hundred yards away.

Moments later, the soldiers were seated on their horses at the rim of a shallow arroyo bordered on the opposite side by a granite ledge. At the bottom was the rocky bed of an ephemeral stream. A series of pools left over from a previous rain stretched along a length of the streambed. Erickson led his command to the water and allowed men and horses to drink their fill and rest.

Two troopers at the end of the column made their way up the arroyo to a small pool not already occupied by their companions. They dismounted and filled their canteens while their horses drank their fill. One of the troopers noted shiny pebbles glinting at the bottom of the pool. After scooping up a handful and examining them, he was stunned to discover they were gold nuggets. His shouts of discovery brought several men to investigate. Moments later, the soldiers were finding more gold in the other pools. Soon, there was a scramble to retrieve the nuggets, the purpose of their mission temporarily forgotten. As Erickson fought to maintain order, another trooper, while investigating the granite ledge close to the stream, announced the discovery of a seam of gold-laden quartz from which nuggets were easily plucked.

Half of the cavalrymen petitioned Erickson to allow them to remain and harvest the gold. Erickson scolded them, reminded them of their assignment, and ordered all onto their horses. Grudgingly, the troopers complied, and an hour later the company filed out of the arroyo and continued westward. Several of the cavalrymen had filled their pockets with nuggets. As the troopers rode away from the arroyo, they searched the surrounding countryside for some distinguishing landmarks, but all was flat, creosote-bush-studded desert.

Two days later, the tracks of the escaping Apaches were encountered and followed. Not long afterward, their encampment was spotted. In the dark of night, Erickson deployed his troopers in a circle around the camp, and at dawn Erickson called for the surrender of the Indians. When their quarry saw they had no chance, they threw down their weapons and agreed to return to the reservation. The girl, exhausted and in shock but otherwise unharmed, was rescued. Weeks later, after recuperating from her ordeal at the fort, she was returned to relatives in Indiana.

During the journey back to Fort Tucson, all the troopers could talk about was the discovery of gold in the shallow arroyo. Several requested immediate discharge from the army so they could return and harvest the nuggets. All were denied. On the first day back at the post, three men deserted and rode away in the direction of the gold-filled arroyo, but were soon apprehended and returned to the fort.

Three weeks later, two more troopers decided to take their chances. Around midnight, they stole two horses, some food, and equipment, and rode away from the fort in search of the gold. For days they traveled, trying to recall the route they had taken earlier in pursuit of the Apaches. They had exhausted all but a few mouthfuls of their water supply when they found the arroyo.

Their joy at locating the source of the gold was replaced with dismay when they discovered that all of the water holes were dry. For the next three days, they scraped around the bottom of the dry holes, retrieving as much gold as they could. They visited the exposed vein in the granite ledge and chipped out more nuggets. At the end of that time, their saddlebags were filled with gold. The last evening in the arroyo, as the deserters prepared a meal, they were completely out of water. It was with great difficulty that they were able to swallow their food.

The next morning, they rode their overloaded horses out of the arroyo and headed north in hopes of finding water. By midday, the animals were staggering under the weight of men, gear, and gold. Dismounting, the men led the horses for another two miles. When it was clear the animals were struggling with the great load, the deserters began discarding food, gear, guns, and ammunition.

Another day passed, and it was decided to lighten the load of the horses by removing some of the gold and burying it. This done, they continued on. The next day, one of the soldiers collapsed. With difficulty, his partner hoisted him onto his horse and proceeded. After another hour, the horse dropped to the ground, dead. Weakened, the two men lay on the desert floor hoping to regain their strength.

That is how they were found the next day by a cavalry patrol out searching for them. One of the men was dead and the other dying. Before he expired, the deserter informed his would-be rescuers that he and his partner had found the arroyo and the gold. As proof, he told them to open the remaining saddlebag. The sergeant in charge of the patrol found the gold, just as promised.

W. C. JAMESON

The patrol camped on the spot for the night. Their intention was to start back to Fort Tucson in the morning with the dead man and the survivor. When the soldiers awoke at dawn, they discovered the second man had died during the night. The two deserters were buried, and the patrol, carrying the saddlebag full of gold, returned to the fort.

On their eventual discharge from the army, a number of the men who were present when the gold was found in the arroyo attempted to make their way back to it. The remains of at least three were found in the desert. The whereabouts of the others has never been determined.

During the first decade of the 1900s, an old man working as a carpenter in Phoenix took several weeks off each spring. The man was a dependable and skilled worker, never said much, and came to be valued by his employer. Though the old man was often gone for a long time, he was always welcomed back on the job. In 1911, the employer expressed his curiosity about the extended time off and asked the old man where he went. The carpenter explained that he traveled into the desert near the Baboquivari Mountains in the southern part of Pima County in search of a rich deposit of gold. Under further questioning, the old man said that during the 1870s, he had been a member of a cavalry troop that stopped at a remote arroyo to water men and horses while pursuing renegade Apaches. The soldiers had discovered gold in abundance in the arroyo, and the old man said that every year since he had been discharged from the army, he reentered the region in hopes of relocating it.

In 1915, the old man returned to Phoenix from his annual trek into the desert in search of the gold. He sought out his employer and gave his resignation. The contractor asked him if he had found the gold. The old man responded by pulling a small bag out of his pocket and spilling several dozen small nuggets onto the man's desk. He told his employer that he would be returning to retrieve more of the gold in a few days.

The old man was never seen again. Many believe he perished in the desert, perhaps another victim of dehydration.

If the reports of the troopers who initially found gold in the remote arroyo in the 1870s were true, then somewhere in the Sonoran Desert, not far from the Baboquivari Mountains, lies a rich ledge of almost pure gold. Men have perished in search of it, and men continue to look for it to this day.

Hidden Gold
in Colossal Cave

During the first week of June 1884, a Southern Pacific passenger train stopped at the small community of Pantano, Arizona, twenty miles southeast of Tucson. Here, it was to take on water and two passengers. The train was making its weekly run from Willcox to Tucson. In addition to passengers, it was transporting $62,000 in gold coins. The money was part of the payroll for federal troops stationed at Fort Lowell near Tucson. The fort had been established eighteen years earlier and served as a supply depot as well as a base of operations for the U.S. Cavalry against hostile Apache Indians. Pantano was founded in 1880. It is now a ghost town.

As the engineer and brakeman filled the water tank, four men wearing masks approached the express car. Prepared to set a charge of dynamite to blow an entrance hole, the bandits were surprised to discover the door had been pushed open and the two Wells Fargo agents guarding the gold were seated at a low table, playing cards.

With drawn revolvers, the bandits climbed into the express car, disarmed the guards, and tied them up. This done, they grabbed the heavy canvas bags containing the gold coins, stuffed them in their saddlebags, and rode away. The outlaws had traveled only two miles when their horses grew tired from the heavy loads of gold. They slowed to a walk, and it became clear that the exhausted animals would not be able to travel much farther. Every few minutes, the bandits would scan the trail behind them to make certain they were not being pursued.

Word of the robbery reached Pima County sheriff Robert Leatherwood at Tucson an hour after the event. Realizing the need for haste, he recruited a posse and galloped toward Pantano. The trail left by the train robbers was clear, and Leatherwood wasted no time in pursuit. It soon became apparent that the bandits were making their way toward the Rincon Mountains.

After several miles, the posse arrived at the house of a rancher named Crane. As they rode up to the front door, Crane stepped out and introduced himself. Without preamble, Crane told the sheriff that the horse thieves he was chasing were headed northward. Leatherwood explained that they were in pursuit not of horse thieves, but of four men who had robbed the Southern Pacific train at Pantano.

Crane then stated that four men had come to his house early that morning and asked if they could exchange their tired horses for some fresh ones. Crane told them he had no mounts to spare. At that point, one of the riders pulled a revolver and pointed it at the rancher. Calmly, the gunman told Crane that they were going to leave the horses they were riding and take four fresh ones. If the rancher resisted, he was informed, he would be shot dead.

As Crane looked on, the four men placed their saddles and bridles onto the fresh horses. During the process, Crane noticed that each of them had difficulty with their saddlebags, which appeared to be heavily loaded. After the four rode away, Crane saddled his only remaining horse and followed them for several miles, keeping well behind. Crane noticed that the horses appropriated by the four men were already tiring, and he suspected it was from the heavy loads they were transporting.

Crane watched from a distance as the riders pulled into a cluster of trees in the forest and dismounted. After tying off the horses, they removed the saddlebags and carried them for several yards until they were out of sight behind some rocks. Crane contemplated trying to recover his horses, but being outnumbered and outarmed, decided it was too risky. He returned to his ranch. Crane pointed toward the trail taken by the robbers, and moments later Leatherwood and the posse were riding in pursuit.

Four hours later, the lawmen arrived in the foothills of the Rincon Mountains and found the place where Crane had seen the bandits tie off the horses. Much to Leatherwood's surprise, the horses were still there. With caution, the lawmen dismounted, pulled their revolvers, and approached the animals. They found no sign of the outlaws. As the possemen unsaddled the horses and led them to some nearby grass to graze, one of them spotted the opening to a cave a short distance away.

One of the deputies approached the dark entrance, weapon in hand. Just as he reached it, a shot rang out from inside and a bullet struck near his foot. Leatherwood called for his men to retreat behind some boulders. Huddled behind the rock, the sheriff explained that since it appeared to be impossible to enter the cave without casualties, they would simply wait out the bandits. According to Crane, the riders were not carrying much in the way of water and food. The posse set up camp a short distance away. Leatherwood sent two men to Tucson for supplies.

Five days passed and nothing came from the cave except silence. After two weeks, Leatherwood decided it was time to enter. He concluded that the robbers had either perished from starvation and thirst or found another way out. With the sheriff in the lead, the posse crept toward the entrance.

Lighting handmade torches, Leatherwood and his men searched the cave but found no sign of habitation. The cavern was long and narrow and contained numerous side passages and small alcoves. After two hours of searching, the sheriff realized the outlaws had somehow escaped. Leatherwood decided the posse should remain in the area and search for any sign of the outlaws.

Two days later, a cowhand rode up to the sheriff's camp. He said he worked for Crane and was looking for stray cattle. After providing the man with a meal and coffee, Leatherwood engaged him in conversation, informing the cowhand of his mission in tracking the train robbers.

The cowhand said it might not mean anything, but just the previous day he had heard reports of four men spending gold coins at the taverns in nearby Willcox. One of the men, according to the cowhand, had openly boasted of robbing a train at Pantano and escaping from a sheriff's posse.

Leatherwood thanked the cowhand for the information. He dismissed the posse and allowed the men to return to their homes in Tucson. An hour later, Leatherwood saddled up and rode to Willcox. At the time, Willcox was little more than a point along the Southern Pacific Railroad tracks where cattle from area ranches were gathered, loaded onto railroad cars, and shipped out. During the few years it had been in existence, a small village of businesses and bars had sprung up.

After riding into Willcox, Leatherwood located the local law-enforcement authorities and told them about the train robbery, the pursuit, and the escape of the outlaws from the cave. After gathering all of the available deputies, the lawmen headed for Railroad Street to search the taverns for the train robbers.

They were located within minutes. After being informed they were under arrest, the bandits decided to shoot it out with the lawmen. The

W. C. JAMESON

combination of too much liquor and getting no sleep for days was their downfall. During the ensuing gunfight, three of the outlaws were killed. The survivor, Phillip Carver, was tried for his part in the train robbery and sentenced to twenty-eight years in the Yuma Territorial Prison.

During interrogation, Carter was asked how he and the other outlaws had managed to escape from the cave. He explained that after two days of searching, one of his companions located a small opening several hundred yards from the main entrance. After hiding the gold coins, they crawled out and made their way to Willcox.

Leatherwood proposed a deal to Carver. He said that if the surviving bandit would lead authorities to the gold coins, he would be given a reduced sentence. Carver told Leatherwood he had no idea where the coins were hidden. He said they were cached during a time he was standing guard near the main entrance to the cave. He just assumed they would all escape and then return sometime in the future to retrieve and divide the gold. It never occurred to him, he said, to ask about where it was cached.

During his prison term, Carver was visited several times by Wells Fargo and other law-enforcement agents who queried him about the gold coins. On each occasion, he told the same story of not being present when the gold was hidden.

Wells Fargo agents went to the cave and searched for the gold, but with no success. Though he stuck to the same story, the agents were convinced that Carver did, in fact, know where the gold was cached. Years later, when Carver was released from prison, he was followed by Wells Fargo agent James Westphal in the hope that the outlaw would lead him to the gold. Westphal tailed Carver to Tucson, where the ex-prisoner took up lodging in a rooming house. After three weeks, Carver vanished.

Westphal assumed Carver would head straight to the cave and retrieve the gold, so the agent traveled to the site and waited. He remained in a small, unobtrusive camp for three weeks, but saw no sign of Carver or anyone else. In fact, Carver was never seen again.

The cave in which the gold coins were cached is known today as Colossal Cave. Old-timers in the Pima County area still refer to it as the Train Robbers' Cave. It is a prominent attraction visited by thousands each year and is located in Pima County Park. According to documents, approximately forty miles of passageways have been explored and mapped to date. The gold, if found today, would have a value of close to three-quarters of a million dollars.

The Lost
Adams Placer

During the past century and a half, few lost mines have lured as many hopeful treasure hunters as the one called the Lost Adams Diggings, one of the richest placer mines in history. During the 1860s, a party of miners arrived at a mysterious canyon sacred to the Apaches and harvested gold nuggets the size of hen's eggs. Most of them died for it. Because of the Indian threat, the location was avoided for a number of years. By the time peace was restored in the region and men attempted to relocate the mine, there was confusion as to the exact location of the canyon. Early writers placed it in western New Mexico on the basis of unsubstantiated information, but a full and logical analysis of the initial discovery reveals that this would be impossible. In truth, the location of the Lost Adams Diggings is in southeastern Arizona. The canyon, complete with all of the pertinent landmarks and identifying features, has been found, and gold aplenty has been taken from the narrow stream that winds through it. What remains lost is the exposed vein of gold that contributed to the rich float found in the creek.

The man known as Adams whose name is given to the famous lost placer mine remains an enigmatic figure. He once admitted to having been born in Rochester, New York, on July 10, 1829, but revealed little else of his background. Even his first name has been lost or forgotten.

What is known is that Adams drove a freight wagon and delivered goods from Los Angeles, California, to Tucson, Arizona, and back. By all accounts, he was a loyal employee and good at his job.

During August 1864, Adams dropped off a load of freight in Tucson, collected a $2,000 payment, and started back on the road to California.

He drove a wagon and trailer filled with a new shipment of goods, and led a string of twelve horses. A few days after leaving Tucson, he stopped along the side of the road near the tiny settlement of Gila Bend and set up camp for the night. Before turning in, Adams set the horses loose to graze on the grasses that grew lush along the floodplain of the nearby Gila River.

Just before dawn, Adams was awakened by a noise. Rising from his blankets, he spotted half a dozen young Apaches running off with his horses. Adams buckled on his gun belt, grabbed his rifle, and pursued on foot. An hour later he caught up with the horse thieves in an arroyo where they had halted to rest. As the Indians tended to the stolen horses, they were unaware of Adams's arrival. The freighter took cover near some rocks and fired his rifle at the Apaches, killing two and driving away the others.

After recovering the horses, Adams herded them back to the campsite, only to discover his wagon and trailer afire and parts of his shipment scattered across the ground. The theft of the horses, he realized, was a diversion so his camp could be robbed.

With the herd of horses, Adams made his way several miles to a Pima village he had passed the previous day. There, he intended to trade a few of the animals for enough supplies to get him back to California.

Still a mile from the Indian village, Adams encountered a party of twenty miners who were panning for gold in a nearby stream. They told the freighter they were on their way to California to try their luck in the goldfields and were hoping to find enough placer gold at this site to fund the remainder of their journey. The miners were traveling on foot, and a few of them professed interest in purchasing some of Adams's horses. As Adams bartered with the miners, a young Mexican dressed in the garb of an Apache arrived to watch the proceedings.

For the rest of the day, the Mexican followed Adams around the miners' camp, and later at the Pima village. During an evening meal, the young man told Adams that he and his brother had been stolen from their family by Apaches on a raid deep in Mexico and carried north to Arizona. His brother was eventually killed by a member of the tribe. He said he had recently been abandoned by the Apaches near this very Pima village, where he had been taken in and treated well. On the right side of his head, the Mexican sported a deformed ear that resembled a piece of knotted rope. The Pimas had given him the name "Gotch Ear."

Each time one of the miners rejoiced at finding a tiny amount of gold in the bottom of the little stream they were panning, Gotch Ear reacted with amusement. When Adams expressed curiosity, the Mexican replied that he knew of a canyon where so much gold could be gathered in a single day that a stout mule would not be able to carry it all. The canyon, he said, was sacred to the Apaches, and was a two-week ride from where they now camped. Gotch Ear went on to explain that he had seen gold nuggets as large as grapes lying at the bottom of the narrow stream that flowed through the canyon.

The next day, Adams related Gotch Ear's story to the miners. All grew excited about the possibilities of locating this gold-filled canyon and asked Adams to negotiate with Gotch Ear to lead them to the gold. Following a brief conversation, the Mexican agreed to lead the men to the canyon in exchange for one of the horses, a saddle, a rifle, and some ammunition.

On the morning of August 20, Adams and the miners, led by Gotch Ear, rode out of the Pima village on their way to the canyon of gold. During the long journey, Adams made an attempt to note landmarks. Years later, it was learned that Adams had a poor sense of direction and distance and was unable to remember much of the country he had passed through. His inability to recall pertinent details of the route was to plague him for most of his life.

Adams said that the party passed near Mounts Ord and Thomas, as well as the White Mountains, and crossed two large rivers—most likely, he said, the Black and the Little Colorado. Since Adams had never been to that part of the country before, it is unclear how he arrived at these conclusions. At one point, the miners crossed a well-used wagon road that Gotch Ear claimed led to Fort Wingate to the north. Given the amount of time the party traveled with loaded horses over rough terrain, it is inconceivable that they could have arrived at a point south of Fort Wingate in western New Mexico. Furthermore, research shows that no such road existed in 1864.

One evening, after two weeks of travel, Gotch Ear led the party to a campsite a short distance from a freshwater spring. The next morning, he told Adams that they were close to the canyon of gold and warned him they were now in the territory of the feared Apache chief Nana. The Apaches, he said, often camped in the very canyon they were about to enter. Nana and his band were known to attack and slay white travelers who passed through his homeland.

W. C. JAMESON

As the miners ate breakfast, Adams noted that not far away was a small irrigated patch of land on which grew pumpkins, squash, and corn. Gotch Ear explained that the Apache women tended to the planting and harvesting to supplement game brought in by the tribe's hunters.

After loading the horses, the miners followed Gotch Ear into a canyon one hundred yards to the northeast. The trip through the canyon was slow and difficult owing to the rough and rocky terrain. Presently, the party arrived at a narrow opening along one wall, a passageway partially hidden by a large boulder. Following the Mexican through the opening, the miners proceeded along a gently sloping trail littered with boulders. A narrow stream wound its way along the bottom of the canyon. Parts of the canyon were so narrow, recalled Adams, that one could touch both walls while riding through it. Adams later described the canyon as Z-shaped.

After a mile, the canyon widened into a small clearing filled with pine trees. Another hundred yards upstream and around a bend was a ten-to-twelve-foot-high waterfall. Beyond the far ridge could be seen the tops of two mountains with rounded peaks. Gotch Ear said the Mexicans called them the Peloncillo Mountains.

As Adams and the miners regarded the little clearing, Gotch Ear pointed to the shallow, slow-moving stream and told them that was where they would find the gold. Though exhausted from the difficult travel, the miners grabbed their gold pans and began swishing the bottom sands through the water. Moments later, excited shouts came from the men as they harvested nuggets from the creek with every dip of a pan.

Two days later, as the miners filled ore bags with gold nuggets, flake, and dust, Gotch Ear told Adams he was ready to leave. After he was presented with the horse and goods he bargained for, Adams and the miners bade him goodbye and wished him a good journey. The Mexican rode away and was never seen again. Months later, Adams learned that one of Nana's warriors was seen riding the horse that had been given to the Mexican.

During the next few days, as more gold was accumulated, Adams fell into the role of leader of the group. At his suggestion, the miners agreed to gather all of the gold mined thus far, store it in a common location, and divide it equally at a later date.

When not panning for gold, the miners busied themselves with the construction of a log cabin to provide shelter against the coming winter.

At one end of the cabin, a large rock hearth was constructed. A hidden chamber was added to the hearth, and into this was placed the growing accumulation of gold.

At one point during the construction of the cabin, the miners were visited by chief Nana and two dozen mounted and armed warriors. Addressing Adams, Nana demanded an explanation for the presence of white men in his valley. Adams told the chief they only wished to pan for gold and that they represented no threat to the Indians. Nana acknowledged that the gold was of little use to him, and told the whites they could remain if they promised to respect the valley and the water. He cautioned them not to overhunt the wild game. Nana also issued a stern warning against trespassing into the upper part of the valley beyond the waterfall, a portion of the canyon he called Sno-ta-hay. The area was sacred, he said, and if anyone violated the agreement, all would be killed.

Weeks passed and provisions ran low. Adams decided to send a party of eight men to the nearest settlement for food, ammunition, and other supplies. Adams later stated that the men traveled to Fort Wingate. A miner named John Brewer was placed in charge of the small expedition. Brewer told Adams it would take about eight days to make the trip.

With the Brewer party gone, the rest of the miners continued to pan gold from the little stream. It appeared to them that there was no end to the wealth of gold nuggets and dust to be found in the sand and gravel. Adams estimated they had collected just over $100,000 worth, all of which was placed in the hearth's secret chamber. As the miners worked, they spotted Indians watching them from the ridges from time to time.

Four days after the Brewer party departed, one of the miners showed Adams a gold nugget the leader later described as "big as a hen's egg." When Adams asked where it had been found, the miner told him he had gathered several of them from the creek just above the waterfall. Adams reminded him and the other miners of Nana's warning and cautioned them to refrain from entering the sacred grounds of the Apache lest harm befall them.

Unknown to Adams, five of the miners, lured by the promise of the large gold nuggets, snuck out of camp that night and panned the stream above the waterfall. The next morning, one of them showed Adams a coffeepot filled with the gold he had obtained from the site. He gave one of the largest nuggets to Adams. Adams repeated Nana's warning, but

W. C. JAMESON

the other miners, on seeing the large nuggets, grabbed their pans and scrambled upstream to retrieve more of them.

On the afternoon of the eighth day following Brewer's departure, Adams grew worried. When the party failed to appear the following morning, Adams and a miner named Davidson rode into the zigzag canyon in hopes of meeting their companions returning with supplies. By the time the two men reached the narrow opening, Adams's worst fears were realized. Scattered across the ground near the entrance were the scalped and mutilated bodies of their friends. Littering the rocky ground among the bodies was what remained of the supplies. On reaching this point during their return trip, Adams realized, the party had been attacked by Apaches.

Now concerned that their companions at the diggings might be facing danger, Adams and Davidson raced back up the canyon to warn them. On approaching the clearing, however, they heard gunshots, the frightened shouts of the miners, and the war cries of the Apaches. From their hiding place among the rocks and brush, Adams and Davidson watched as three hundred mounted Indians rode up and down the clearing near the cabin, killing the miners one by one. After the dead men had been scalped and dismembered, the cabin was set afire.

Fearing they might be discovered, Adams and Davidson dismounted and crawled into the cover of some heavy brush and waited for the Indians to finish their grisly business and leave. Just before sundown, the Apaches rode away toward the waterfall. When they felt certain the Indians were gone, Adams and Davidson crept from their hiding place to the cabin with the intention of retrieving the gold hidden in the hearth. On arriving, however, the intense heat from the still-smoldering embers prevented them from reaching the nuggets. Fearing that the Apaches might return, the two men returned to their horses, mounted up, and rode back down the canyon and out of the range. The only gold in their possession was the large nugget given to Adams earlier, which he carried in a pocket.

Days later, Adams and Davidson, having not eaten since leaving the canyon, killed one of their horses and cooked the meat from a haunch. Riding double on the remaining animal, they were discovered two weeks later by a cavalry patrol from Fort Apache. The two survivors were escorted to the post and admitted to the hospital, where they were treated for malnutrition and exhaustion. Davidson, who was in his fifties and in poor health, died several days later.

Adams was never the same after his ordeal. After being sent to Fort Wingate to recover, he obtained a pistol and shot two young Apaches who were working as scouts. Adams insisted they were among the raiders who had slaughtered the miners. Adams was charged with murder. While confined to the Fort Wingate jail, a sympathetic officer allowed him to escape. Fleeing westward, Adams stopped in Tucson long enough to sell the gold nugget he carried. From there he proceeded to Los Angeles, where he was reunited with his wife and three children.

For the next ten years, Adams suffered horrible nightmares in which he relived the ordeal of watching his friends being attacked, killed, and mutilated by the Apaches in the canyon of gold. Though he knew that a great fortune awaited him should he return to the canyon and the diggings, he could not bring himself to do so for fear of encountering Chief Nana and his warriors.

A retired ship captain named C. A. Shaw learned the story of the Adams party and the canyon of gold. Shaw was intrigued with the idea of finding the canyon. He located Adams in California and offered to finance an expedition. He asked Adams to guide it. Adams, now forty-five years old, was hesitant, but finally agreed to the proposition. During the expedition, Adams became lost dozens of times and was unable to recognize any pertinent landmarks. His inability to determine distance and direction became obvious to Shaw. During the next decade, Shaw undertook several more expeditions, each time with Adams serving as guide. Each time, they became lost and returned unsuccessful.

The Fort Wingate physician who had treated Adams years earlier became interested in finding the canyon of gold as a result of hearing his patient's provocative tale. Using the few details and directions provided by Adams, the doctor ventured into the rugged mountain ranges of southwestern New Mexico and southeastern Arizona in search of the diggings. The doctor, never much of an outdoorsman, suffered from the rigors of the search and gave up after a few attempts. In turn, he told his story to a man named John Dowling.

Dowling was an experienced miner and commercial hunter, and no stranger to the wilderness. He also had some experience with the mountain range in which he believed the lost Adams placer to be located, having successfully panned gold from many of the small streams found in the nearby canyons. One day, Dowling found himself riding through a

W. C. JAMESON

narrow Z-shaped canyon that widened into a small clearing. Here, he found over sixty tree stumps. A short distance away, he came to an old pile of ash and charcoal and the remains of a stone hearth and chimney. At the time, Dowling knew nothing of the cache of gold nuggets lying in the hearth. For several days, Dowling panned the narrow stream that ran through the canyon and recovered a small amount of gold. He left the canyon, never to return.

While in New Mexico one year while searching for the lost canyon, Adams met a man named Bob Lewis in the town of Magdalena. Lewis told Adams he had been searching for the lost placer mine, but with no success. Using information provided by Adams, Lewis then concentrated his search on the nearby Datil Mountains—where, he claimed, he found it.

Lewis claimed he had located the entrance to a zigzag canyon. On entering it, he said he found the skeletal remains of a number of men and horses, which he concluded were those of the Brewer party. Lewis entered the valley and panned for gold in the narrow stream. Finding barely enough to fill a small poke, he left. For the rest of his life, Lewis boasted of being the man who found the Lost Adams Diggings in the Datil Mountains.

During the summer of 1888, a man accompanied by his wife and daughter pulled up to the ranch house of John Tenney, located on the west flank of the Datil Mountains. Trailing behind the wagon was a herd of twenty cattle and a few horses. After introducing himself to Tenney, the man requested permission to camp nearby and rest and graze his tired and hungry stock for a few days. Tenney agreed and pointed toward a suitable location a quarter mile distant.

Later that evening, Tenney rode over to the campsite to visit with the travelers. The newcomer introduced himself as John Brewer. Tenney, who knew the tale of what was being called the Lost Adams Diggings, asked if he was the same John Brewer who had accompanied Adams to the fateful canyon. The newcomer admitted he was.

For the rest of the evening, Brewer told Tenney his version of the events that had taken place twenty-four years earlier. Though badly wounded, Brewer and two of his companions had managed to escape from the Apaches during the attack at the mouth of the narrow canyon. They rode westward into the desert where, tired and hungry, they were taken in by friendly Indians. It took Brewer three months to recover.

He never learned what happened to his two friends. Though tempted to return to the canyon to retrieve the gold, Brewer could not bring himself to do so, believing the region was cursed. He told Tenney there was more gold in that lost canyon than ten kings could spend in a lifetime.

The Lost Adams Diggings has been the subject of hundreds of searches. More than a dozen different locations have been identified as possible sites. During the past century and more, most of the searches have been directed in the area of the Datil Mountains, mostly based on the widely printed tales of Bob Lewis.

A careful study of the journey of Adams's party from the Pima Indian village to the canyon of gold in 1864, however, would render the Datil Mountains an unlikely location. Given the fact that the party traveled for no more than two weeks, and probably less, and given the fact that they traveled via foot and packed horses over poor-to-nonexistent roads through extremely rough, mountainous country, there is little probability that they ever got out of Arizona. Further, given Adams's well-known inability to recall or understand distances and directions, one must disregard his observations. If one ignores the exaggerated tales that have been written about the many potential locations of the Lost Adams Diggings and applies some inductive and deductive logic, one returns time and again to a region in southeastern Arizona not far from the town of Morenci.

During the 1990s, a Colorado resident who had long studied the story of the Lost Adams Diggings traveled to a location near the Arizona–New Mexico border not far from Morenci. There, he found a narrow Z-shaped canyon similar to the one described by Adams. Some distance up the canyon, he found a clearing, in the middle of which was an old cabin, the type used by cowhands. The shack was built atop the charred remains of an earlier structure. At one end of the cabin was an old, tumbled-down stone hearth and chimney. In the hearth was found a hidden chamber. It was empty.

One hundred yards upstream, the searcher found a ten-foot-high waterfall. Above and beyond the waterfall, there was a grassy area that could have served as a campground, quite possibly the one Chief Nana claimed. The searcher continued up the tiny canyon and near the top could see two cone-shaped mountains in the distance.

Subsequent trips to, and research on, the canyon revealed that gold

W. C. JAMESON

had been found there. It was learned that during the construction of Arizona State Highway 191, the road crews would take their lunch in the shade found in the canyon. One day, one of them discovered gold in the narrow stream that ran along the bottom. The men quit their road-construction jobs and, for weeks thereafter, panned gold from the stream.

Further research revealed that over the years, a few people who knew about this gold-laden stream would arrive on weekends and pan for gold, sometimes leaving with a quart jar half filled with nuggets.

In 2006, the entrance to the canyon was fenced off, and a sophisticated gold-mining operation involving heavy equipment and machinery was installed at its mouth. The operation, overseen by a nearby copper-mining corporation, has been systematically and successfully removing a significant amount of gold.

What remains a mystery, however, is the source of the gold float that is found in the stream. Somewhere farther up the canyon, above and beyond the waterfall, lies an exposed vein of rich gold. Over time, the ore weathers from the rock, is carried downslope by gravity, and is deposited in the streambed.

The stream, at least in the canyon, has for the most part been panned out. At one time, however, it may have been the richest placer mine in the history of the United States. The Lost Adams Diggings is lost no more, but the vein of gold that led to the formation of this now legendary mine still remains to be found.

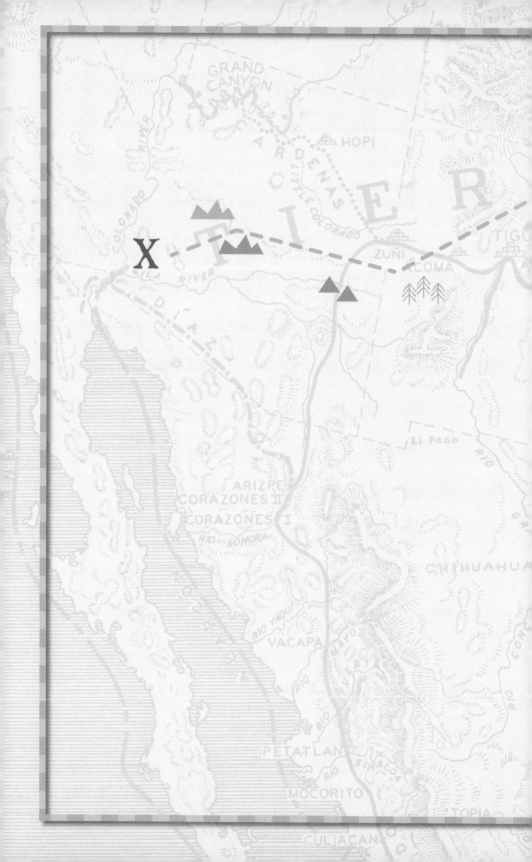

Southwest

Private Flannigan's Lost Gold

In 1869, Private Eugene Flannigan was a member of a U.S. Cavalry detachment stationed at a temporary camp near Gila Bend in southwestern Arizona. During the last week of June, Flannigan and his fellow cavalrymen were ordered to take up pursuit of a small band of Apaches that had kidnapped the young daughter of a settler and fled toward the Gila Bend Mountains to the northwest. As a result of an unanticipated set of circumstances, Flannigan discovered a rich source of gold. That he found a significant deposit of ore has never been questioned, for fifty pounds of it was harvested and seen by others. When Flannigan died, however, the location of the gold became lost and remains so today.

Abner McKeever was grateful for the abundance of rainfall the desert had received during the final week of June. As he walked out into his field near the great bend of the Gila River to examine the beginnings of a healthy yield of corn, squash, and beans, he said a prayer of thanks. McKeever carried a hoe and was accompanied by his wife, son, and daughter. He thought it was a good day to thin some of the plants and dig out some weeds. Near the house, horses milled in the corral, perhaps anticipating the bounty they would share in the coming weeks.

As the family walked between the rows, they were suddenly surprised by a dozen mounted Apaches, who appeared over a low rise in the distance and were galloping toward them. At first, McKeever ordered his family back to the house, but realized they would never reach it before being overtaken by the Indians. He threw down his hoe, gathered his family behind him, and pulled a pistol from his belt, determined to stand off the attackers.

It was over in a few seconds. McKeever and his wife were wounded, and his son lay dead on the ground. His eight-year-old daughter, Belle, was grabbed by an Apache and pulled onto his mount, a captive. After taking the horses from the corral, the Indians rode away in the direction from which they had come.

Bleeding badly, McKeever rode to a neighbor's ranch three miles away and informed him of the attack. The neighbor, in turn, rode to a nearby encampment of cavalry and alerted them. The soldiers, along with some volunteers from Gila Bend, set out in pursuit of the Apaches with hopes of rescuing the little girl. About one mile north of the McKeever farm, tracks showed that the party of Indians had broken up into several groups and set out in different directions. Likewise, the pursuers split up into small groups, each one following a trail.

One small detachment, consisting of Sergeant Crossthwaite and Privates Joe Wormley and Eugene Flannigan, took up the trail that led into the Gila Bend Mountains to the northwest. After a few miles, the Apaches crossed bare rock and the pursuers lost the trail. All three soldiers were new to the desert, unskilled at tracking, and poorly prepared to deal with Indians should they encounter them.

About an hour before sunset, the three men found themselves not only lost but out of water. Dark found them riding in a northwesterly direction in hopes of encountering a stream or spring. All night long they rode in the heart of the small range, and dawn found them and their mounts exhausted, hungry, and thirsty. Suddenly, Private Wormley pointed in the direction of a sparse cluster of low-growing trees in a depression just ahead. The soldiers rode toward it and rejoiced in finding a pool of clear, cool water formed by a gurgling spring.

Apaches were the last thing on the minds of the three men as they drank of the life-giving water. After the horses quenched their thirst, they were unsaddled, hobbled, and turned loose to graze on the grasses that grew along the tiny stream that ran from the pool. The three men decided to remain at the spring for at least a day, resting up from their ordeal, and then attempt to rejoin their company. They dozed in the shade of the trees, and for a while, all seemed well. Shortly before evening, as preparations were being made for supper, Wormley experienced seizures and began raving and screaming. Crossthwaite and Flannigan did what they could for their companion, but Wormley remained delirious.

Following dinner, Flannigan carried the dishes and cups to the little

W. C. JAMESON

pool to wash them and to fill the canteens. As he rinsed them in the clear water, he spied a reflected glint of color at the bottom. Reaching into the water, he scooped up a handful of pebbles and examined them closely. He was astonished to discover several large nuggets of gold among them. More handfuls yielded more nuggets, and soon Flannigan was stuffing the ore into his shirt pockets.

On a hunch, Flannigan abandoned the dishes and explored around the pool, particularly the rock outcrop on the opposite side. Here, several feet above the spring, he found the source of the gold in the pool: two veins of gold-laden quartz, one five inches wide, the other sixteen inches wide. With his pocketknife, he easily carved out several more pieces of the soft ore.

Minutes later, Flannigan returned to camp and told Crossthwaite about his discovery. The two men returned to the rock outcrop and dug out more of the exposed gold, collecting a total of fifty pounds before it grew too dark to work any longer. They returned to camp and placed the gold in their saddlebags.

The following morning, Wormley was still delirious and had to be tied onto his horse. After filling the canteens, the three men set out in a southeasterly direction, hoping to reach the town of Gila Bend within two days. Evening of the second day found them hopelessly lost, so they set up camp alongside the road they followed. The next morning, they decided to split up, believing they would have a better chance of surviving. After tying Wormley to his saddle and securing the mount to his own with a rope, Crossthwaite mounted up and headed east. Flannigan rode south. It was agreed that the first to encounter help would organize a search for the other. That night, Crossthwaite made camp, staked out the horses, and helped Wormley into his bedroll. The next morning, however, Wormley and his horse were nowhere to be seen.

A short time later, a platoon of cavalry found Wormley. He was lying on the bank of the Gila River, sick and raving and unable to tell the soldiers anything about his companions. He was returned to his company, but never regained his sanity.

Around noon, another platoon encountered Flannigan's horse dead on the trail. Noting that the soldier's footprints led away from the animal, they followed them. Several hours later, they rode up on Flannigan lying in the middle of the road. At first, they thought he was dead, but when they examined him found he had only passed out. From his clutching fingers they pulled a saddlebag that was filled with gold nuggets.

Flannigan woke the next morning inside a medical tent at the cavalry encampment. When he asked about Crossthwaite, he was told that the sergeant had been found the previous day, dead. They had returned his body to the camp along with his gold-nugget-filled saddlebag. The gold from Flannigan's and Crossthwaite's saddlebags yielded $1,800.

The next day, Flannigan met with his commanding officer and told him about his ordeal and the discovery of the gold at the spring in the Gila Bend Mountains. When he described the location of the spring, none of the men who heard the story were familiar with any of the landmarks. While Flannigan recovered from his ordeal, the search for Belle McKeever continued, lasting six weeks. She was never found.

Eugene Flannigan was discharged from the army several months later. The day after his separation, he outfitted himself for a trip into the Gila Bend range to search for the spring and retrieve enough gold to make him rich. Despite the fact that the country was still at war with the Apaches, and the fact that he would have to retrace his route across a waterless desert, Flannigan was unbowed. Leading two mules strapped with provisions, he rode into the general area where he and Crossthwaite and Wormley had became lost.

Flannigan searched until he ran out of food and water, but he was unable to relocate the spring. He returned to Gila Bend to resupply, and then set out again. For ten years, Flannigan searched for the spring and its accompanying gold outcrop, each time returning empty-handed. By now, the story was well known throughout the desert Southwest, and others had taken up the search for the gold.

One morning in April 1881, Flannigan was purchasing supplies at a Gila Bend trading post in preparation for another trip into the mountains. As he loaded his mules, he visited with friends and merchants, then bade them farewell and rode out of town. It was the last time anyone saw Eugene Flannigan alive.

Around mid-June, his body was discovered by a party of travelers near the northwestern corner of Yuma County, some forty miles northwest of the Gila Bend Mountains. His corpse had been ravaged by coyotes and vultures, and the soles of his boots had been worn paper-thin, suggesting he had walked a long way. Both of his canteens were empty. Aside from a pistol, the only other thing the travelers found was a pair of saddlebags. When they opened them up, they were surprised to find them filled with gold nuggets.

For a decade, Flannigan had searched for his lost spring and its gold. With each trip into the forbidding, arid mountains and desert, he confessed to friends that he wondered if he would ever return. The lure of the gold he knew was there kept him in search of it, kept him on his quest. Then, he found it, and suddenly Eugene Flannigan was a wealthy man. This time, he was lucky. But, he was not lucky enough to escape the desert to enjoy his newfound wealth.

Over a century later, treasure hunters continue to search for Flannigan's lost gold in the Gila Bend Mountains. It has not been found, but in the general area, several productive gold mines have been established. As in the days when the Apaches roamed this area, the waterless, dry, scorching-hot desert takes it toll on all who enter. To date, few have been up to the challenge.

Scalp
Hunter's Gold

Though not exactly a household name, John J. Glanton may have been one of North America's most proficient and effective killers. Glanton is surrounded by several provocative myths. One relates that he transported several mule loads of gold with him wherever he traveled, gold acquired over time as bounty for scalps and from robberies. During an Indian attack on his fortress near Yuma, Glanton hastily buried his fortune. The rich and elusive cache has never been found.

During the late 1840s, John Glanton became a renowned scalp hunter throughout Mexico and the American Southwest. He was also, by all descriptions, a ruthless and cunning bandit. Unlike most bandits of his day, Glanton possessed the unusual ability to hang onto his ill-gotten gains, carefully saving and transporting them with him as he traveled. At the end of ten years of scalp hunting and banditry, Glanton had become a wealthy man.

John Joel Glanton was born in 1819 in Edgefield County, South Carolina. In his early teens, he left home, wandering across the country and getting work where he could find it. He ended up for a time in central and west Texas. At seventeen years of age, he was deemed adept at survival and tracking and was hired by a cavalry officer named Lieutenant Fannin as a scout for the army. After serving in this capacity for several months, Glanton abruptly quit, took a Lipan Apache bride, and settled into a life of farming near the Guadalupe River in Gonzales County. Glanton had only been married six months when he returned home from a hunting trip and found his wife killed, scalped, and mutilated, presumably by Comanches, who were a constant threat in the area.

A short time later, Glanton abandoned his farm and moved to San Antonio. There, he married again, this time to a young woman from a well-to-do Mexican merchant family. For reasons unknown, Glanton abandoned his second wife during the winter of 1847 and enlisted in the U.S. Army. Military records show that Glanton participated in the Snively Expedition, served under General Zachary Taylor, and also rode with Captain Jack Hayes during the war with Mexico. Glanton was described as a fearless soldier and ready to fight at a moment's notice. Unfortunately, he fought with his fellow soldiers as often as with the enemy. While on duty in Mexico, he was arrested for shooting a citizen during a barroom brawl. After serving one week in the brig, he escaped and fled deep into the Sierra Madres of Chihuahua.

Months later, Glanton resurfaced—this time as a member of a band of scalp hunters in the service of the Mexican government that was led by a ruthless fiend named Santiago Kirker. Because of ongoing and deadly confrontations between Mexicans and Apaches, the government offered a bounty worth the equivalent of $50 in gold for every Apache scalp turned in. In a short time, the small army of scalp hunters attacked dozens of Apache encampments in the Sierras, killing and scalping men, women, and children. The Indians, themselves brave and ferocious fighters, feared Kirker's scalp hunters more than any other enemy. Over time, Glanton accumulated a sizable fortune, which he kept in his saddlebags and guarded intently.

When the scalp hunters were unable to locate Apaches, they killed and scalped Mexicans, turning their hair in for the bounty. When Mexican officials learned of this practice, they issued warrants for Kirker and his cutthroats, and sent soldiers in pursuit of them. In fleeing the Mexican army, the scalp hunters headed northward, eventually crossing the Rio Grande into Texas. During the flight, Glanton and Kirker had a violent argument. Both men drew knives, and during the confrontation, Glanton killed Kirker and assumed the leadership of the band.

Once safe from the pursuing *federales*, Glanton led his charges westward through Texas, New Mexico, and Arizona, then turned south into the Mexican state of Sonora. Glanton soon made the same arrangements with military leaders there: to bring in Apache scalps in exchange for a bounty. During the next several months, the scalp hunters ranged throughout the Sierra Madres, killing and scalping Indians. Their search for scalps carried them northward into Arizona and New Mexico. If

Apaches could not be found, the hunters would attack encampments of Navajos, Hopis, and other tribes. In addition to hunting for scalps, Glanton and his men found freight wagons, stagecoaches, and small towns easy prey and gradually added to their growing wealth. Following a raid, the scalp hunters would often go on a drunken spree, spending their newfound riches on alcohol and women. The more frugal Glanton remained in camp, far from the revelry, counting his money.

As his store of gold grew too large and heavy to be carried in his saddlebags, Glanton began packing it onto a mule. When his fortune grew so large that it took two mules to transport it, it was said that Glanton no longer slept in camp. Instead, he would lead his gold-heavy mules some distance away and stand guard over his wealth throughout the night.

It was during this time that Glanton underwent a change. For the previous two years, the taking of scalps was no more than a business to him, and one that he was good at. Now, however, it was said that Glanton began to take great pleasure in the act of killing, had become obsessed with it. It was reported that he often shot travelers he encountered along the trail just for sport. If someone disagreed with him over some matter, no matter how trivial, Glanton would shoot or stab them. Though never known to be much of a drinker, Glanton began imbibing alcohol frequently, his drunkenness exacerbating his already volatile moods. His wealth grew so rapidly that soon he added a third mule. Then a fourth.

In constant search of Apache scalps, Glanton led his band of killers to a location just south of Tucson, where they set up camp. There were fourteen men in all, half of them Mexican. From this base, the men foraged out, raiding small mining camps and attacking freight wagons, sometimes accumulating thousands of dollars worth of gold nuggets at a time. In retaliation, the miners formed a vigilante group, which launched an attack on Glanton's camp, killing several of the bandits.

The following day, Glanton led his men northwestward to Phoenix, hoping the scalping and raiding opportunities would be greater. Outside Phoenix, they encountered and attacked a peaceful Pima Indian village in hopes of adding to their accumulation of scalps. Surprisingly, the Pimas were well armed and put up a fight, killing or wounding half of Glanton's men and driving them off. As the band of scalp hunters rode away from the Pima village, Glanton personally killed the wounded men so they would not slow down the escape.

The scalp hunters traveled westward, and several weeks later arrived at the small town of Yuma on the east bank of the Colorado River. Within days, Glanton and his men had taken over the town. The year was 1849. At the time there were two ferries operating near Yuma, both transporting goods to and from California across the Colorado River. Both operations proved lucrative, and in a short time Glanton decided to cut himself in on the action. He went into partnership with Able Lincoln, who owned the southernmost ferry. He raised the crossing fee from three dollars to ten. Glanton was also known to rob and murder some travelers who displayed any wealth. In addition, he seized goods that were being moved across the river. Among those seized was a quantity of gold being transported from the rich mines in California to the east. Thus, Glanton's wealth grew even more.

Not desiring the competition from the northernmost ferry, Glanton decided to put it out of business. A short time after Glanton partnered with Lincoln, someone shot and killed the other ferry operator and destroyed the cable.

Glanton decided that operating the ferry boats and stealing the cargo was far more lucrative than riding across the countryside in search of Indian scalps. Anticipating living out his life in Yuma, Glanton ordered the construction of an adobe-walled fortress on a nearby hill overlooking the Colorado River. When completed, he named it Fort Defiance. Glanton and his men moved in, taking with them mistresses from the Mexican population of the town. In addition to running the ferry, Glanton also took over the town's saloon and several other businesses.

For months, men returning from the goldfields in California via the Yuma ferry were systematically robbed and killed, their bodies tossed into the river. In this manner, Glanton added to his already extensive wealth. During this time, he was regarded by many as the wealthiest man in the American Southwest. And the craziest.

As Glanton grew richer, gained more power, and drank heavily, he became more insane. Even his men, all ruthless, trail-hardened killers, began to fear his unpredictable and wild moods. One by one they deserted, and soon he was left alone behind the walls and locked doors of the fortress. Even his woman abandoned him, and in solitude, with nothing but his gold, he remained at Fort Defiance for weeks at a time. When he did appear in town, he was described as appearing unkempt, with long, stringy hair and filthy, ragged clothes. In one hand he carried a loaded pistol, in the other a long-bladed hunting knife. Glanton, it was said, had become a maniac.

One day, a young boy went to Fort Defiance to warn Glanton that a force of Yuma Indians was approaching from the north and appeared intent on attacking the town. In his crazed state of mind, Glanton was convinced the Indians were after his gold. He decided to hide the treasure.

During the remainder of the day, Glanton worked feverishly, gathering up his fortune in Mexican and American gold coins, gold nuggets, jewelry, and some currency. Some researchers insist that Glanton never left the fort, and thus his wealth must be buried somewhere within the limits of the walls. Others maintain that Glanton, leading one mule at a time, made several trips from the fortress and into the nearby sandhills, where he buried his fortune.

Whatever the truth, the Yuma Indians attacked the town the following morning. Encountering very little resistance, they stole goods and burned most of the buildings. Still in a murderous frenzy, they turned their attention to Fort Defiance on the hill. They broke through the gates, took what they could find, and set fire to the buildings. When the Indians finally rode away, several curious Yuma citizens entered the fortress. They found Glanton's body, scalped and mutilated. A preliminary search throughout the structure for Glanton's fortune yielded nothing.

During the next few months, as the news of Glanton's death spread throughout the area, men arrived to search for his buried treasure, which was estimated to be worth untold millions. Hundreds of holes were dug inside the fortress, to no avail. Hundreds more were excavated just outside the walls, again with no success. The treasure seekers ranged into the sandhills, searching for some sign of recent burial. More holes were dug, but success was not to be had.

Following Glanton's death, a Yuma resident, an old man named Collins, assumed control of the ferry operation. With the passage of years, Collins befriended an aged Yuma Indian who had taken up residence in the town. During a conversation with the old Indian, Collins learned that he had participated in the attack on the town and Fort Defiance years earlier. When Collins asked the Indian what he knew about Glanton's fortune in gold, the Yuma related an interesting story.

The Indian told Collins that just before the attack on the town, he and several other Indians were camped not far from Fort Defiance. They were to assess the strength and numbers of the people in the town and

W. C. JAMESON

report back to the chief. While they were encamped, they observed Glanton make several trips from the fortress in the dark of night, each time leading a heavily laden mule. They watched as Glanton dug a number of holes in the sand dunes just south of the fort and next to the river. Glanton deposited his wealth into these holes, covered them up, and returned to the fort.

According to the Indian, after Glanton departed and before the Indians were to break camp and return to their chief, they stole over to where the treasure was buried, dug up all of the gold, and threw it into the Colorado River.

If what the old Yuma Indian said was true, then Glanton's incredible fortune still lies close by, buried under the sand and silt of the river. Gold, being of high specific gravity, undoubtedly sank through the bottom sands and silts and was not transported any significant distance.

If what the Indian said was true, the gold is still there in the river bottom close to the bank. Its value is estimated to be more than ten million dollars.

Lost Gold in the
Little Horn Mountains

Arizona's Little Horn Mountains are located approximately seventy miles northeast of Yuma and twenty-five miles north of the town of Aztec on Interstate 8. In the Little Horns, there is a canyon well known to the Tonto Apaches. It was the source of the gold they used to purchase arms and ammunition for their fight with the U.S. Army. Lying on the floor of this canyon, claim the Indians, are hundreds of red rocks that, when broken open, yield gold.

In 1874, General George Crook forced the surrender of the majority of the Tonto Apaches and marched them to the reservation at Camp Verde, some eighty miles north-northeast of Phoenix. The Indians were provided with tools and taught to plant wheat and corn. This place, they were told, would be their home forever. One year later, however, the Tontos were moved from Camp Verde to the San Carlos Indian Reservation in southeastern Arizona. Over 1,500 Tontos began the journey, but fewer than 1,400 arrived. The rest fled back to their homelands and attempted a new beginning in the arid desert and mountains. The U.S. Cavalry pursued and relentlessly engaged the Indians in battle, eventually apprehending all of the truants. Following the capture of a group of one hundred, the troopers escorted them to the ranch of José Alvarado, where they were held at a camp near the Gila River.

Alvarado rode to the camp one day and introduced himself to the Indians. He found them courteous and rather gentle, and in time came to be friends with them. From time to time, he would cut out a young steer, deliver it to the camp, and have it butchered so they would have fresh meat.

One of the Indians who grew close to Alvarado was named Pancho.

Sometimes in the evenings, Alvarado and Pancho would sit beside a campfire and smoke while talking about the days of early settlement in the area. With time, the Tontos were moved off the Alvarado ranch and transported to the San Carlos Reservation.

Months later, Pancho, along with his wife and young son, appeared at the home of José Alvarado. Pancho explained that he had left the reservation because he could not stand the heat and sickness that permeated the location. He asked Alvarado for a job and was put to work.

One afternoon, Pancho's son came down with a sickness. Alvarado carried the boy to a nearby mission and turned him over to the priest to be cared for. The boy recovered, and Pancho allowed him to be baptized. He told Alvarado that he owed him a great debt and someday would repay him with riches beyond his wildest imagination.

In 1891, the Gila River flooded and devastated the region. Rancher Alvarado lost hundreds of cattle, and his houses and barns were carried away in the floodwaters. Broken and in despair, Alvarado moved his family to Yuma, and Pancho went to work for another rancher.

Before a year had passed, Alvarado was back at his holdings along the Gila River and determined to rebuild. Around this time, gold was discovered in the Harquahala Mountains, fifty miles to the north. Palomas, a small village located near Alvarado's ranch, grew to become an important transfer point for freight destined for the new mine.

Alvarado reestablished his herd and constructed a small home of adobe and logs. While he was happy to be back on his land, he had a difficult time paying his debts and was close to poverty. Around this time, his old friend Pancho visited him. On learning of his friend's difficulties, Pancho told Alvarado it was time for him to pay his overdue debt. Pancho told his friend that he wanted to take him to the richest gold mine in America, and that the gold was lying on the floor of a remote canyon, waiting to be picked up.

Alvarado explained to the Indian that he was old and often ill and found it difficult to travel. Pancho promised to bring him a smooth-riding horse with which to make the journey to the canyon. Alvarado agreed, but insisted on bringing along two of his Mexican ranch hands. On learning of their assignment, the hands became angry and blamed the Indian. A brief argument ensued between them before Alvarado intervened. The hands agreed to go along, but it was clear they were perturbed.

On the morning of departure, Pancho rode in the lead. Behind was

Alvarado, and the ranch hands brought up the rear on foot, leading two burros packed with camping supplies and food. The small party traveled north along the old Kofa–Mohawk freight route that led from the Southern Pacific siding to the Kofa Mine in the Kofa Mountains. They passed the Palomas Mountains and the Tank Mountains on their right. South of the turnoff to the Kofa Mine, they left the road and headed northeast through Engresser Pass.

At the camp that night, the two hired men provoked Pancho into an argument. The next morning, Pancho, distrustful of them, decided not to travel directly to the canyon of gold, but rather led the party north to Alamo Spring. During the morning, he told Alvarado he did not trust his ranch hands and did not want them to know the location of the gold. At Alamo Spring, Alvarado, under instructions from Pancho, told the two hired men they would leave for the ranch in the morning. What he did not tell them was that Pancho would return by a different route so that he could show Alvarado the canyon.

The group camped that night at Alamo Spring and left the following morning along what Alvarado told his men was a back trail. On the trail, Pancho asked to borrow the rancher's rifle, explaining that he was going to ride off a way and hunt some bighorn sheep. Pancho directed Alvarado and the ranch hands to continue eastward along a dry riverbed. At a certain point, he said, they would come to a rock cistern. There they were to wait for him.

Two hours later, Pancho approached the three men seated by the rock cistern. He carried a rock the size of a man's head and threw it on the ground in front of them, instructing Alvarado to bust it open. The rancher examined the rock, noting that it had a red-black surface, the color due to the presence of limonite and hematite—both minerals often associated with gold deposits. Alvarado broke open the rock and was astonished to find the inside rich with gold.

The four men camped that night at the cistern. Before dawn, Pancho woke Alvarado and led him some distance from the camp so he could speak with him. He pointed up the wash he had ridden out of the previous day and told the rancher that about a mile and a half up the wash was a small side wash where many of the red-brown rocks could be seen scattered along the floor. There, said Pancho, was the source of the gold of the Tonto Apaches. When Pancho was certain his friend understood the directions, the two men returned to camp.

W. C. JAMESON

By the time the two ranch hands awoke, Pancho was gone. Alvarado never saw him again. Silently, he thanked his friend who had insisted on repaying his debt. Knowing the location of the gold, Alvarado would return, harvest some of it, and pay off all of his own obligations and build his cattle herd.

It was not to be. One month after returning from the trek, Alvarado died. Before passing, however, he called his son José Jr. to his bedside and told him the entire story of Pancho and the gold. As best he could remember, he related the directions to the small canyon of gold and urged his son to travel to the site and glean as much as he could.

Ranch duties prevented José Jr. from searching for the gold for several years. In 1918, while he was running a dairy, he finally found the time to mount a search. He traveled along the route described by his father, but became lost several times. He was never able to find Alamo Spring or the cistern. He found what he said were dozens of washes, but none of them were littered with the red-brown stones described by his father.

In 1955, Ed Rochester and Harold O. Weight, using the directions obtained from José Alvarado Jr., set out to try to find the gold of the Tontos. They found Alamo Spring noted on several different maps, but each had it in a different location. They sought advice from old-timers in the area, including Burt Hart and Bill Keiser of Quartzite as well as a man named Livingstone who owned a ranch in nearby New Water Pass. With their help, they rode directly to the spring, only to be informed later that they had gone to Upper Alamo Spring and that the one they sought no longer flowed.

Three more days of searching failed to yield the cistern described by Alvarado. While camped one night near the western edge of the Little Horn Mountains, the men made preparations for an intensive hunt in the morning. Following breakfast the next day, they discovered they were camped within one mile of the home of a man named Ray Hovetter. Hovetter held several manganese mining claims in the region. He knew exactly where the rock cistern was located and drew a map for the two men. He said the cistern was linked to Alamo Spring by an old Indian trail. The cistern, he said, was still being used and maintained by some of the miners who worked for him. Not far from the cistern, said Hovetter, a small amount of gold had been discovered during the 1920s.

From the cistern, the searchers hiked up a wash for a mile and a half, where they found a smaller one entering from their right. They explored the smaller wash for an hour, but the intense heat forced them to quit the area before they wanted to. A lack of water and fatigue led to them abandoning the area later that afternoon, but they left heartened that they had found the approximate area of the gold of the Tonto Apaches. Conflicting schedules prevented the searchers from returning. As they were elderly, both men passed away before they had another opportunity.

In 1971, a young man arrived at Yuma with a story to tell. He had been hiking and exploring in the Little Horn Mountains north of Aztec. Being a rock hound, he picked up interesting specimens he found during his explorations. In Yuma, he pulled several golf-ball-sized rocks from his pack to show a friend—rocks with a red-brown surface. He told his friend he had found hundreds of them scattered along the bed of a dry wash, and having never seen any before, he asked the friend what they were. The friend broke one open with a hammer, and to the astonishment of both men, revealed an interior of gold. The second rock yielded the same. And the third.

The hiker returned to the Little Horn Mountains several times during the next ten years in search of the wash containing the red-brown rocks. He was never able to find it.

Somewhere in the Little Horn Mountains, the remote and elusive wash containing the odd gold-filled rocks continues to beckon hopeful searchers.

Lost Gold
of Tule Tank

Tule Tank is a natural basin located in the Tule Mountains just north of the Mexican border in southwestern Arizona. During rainy years, the basin fills with water and serves as a source of moisture for wildlife. Cattails thrive at the shoreline. According to legend, not far from Tule Tank lies a field of gold nuggets so rich that one can walk out and pluck them from the ground with ease.

This tale has its beginnings in the small village of Caborca in the Mexican state of Sonora, about seventy-five miles southeast of the border town of Lukeville. During the mid-1880s, an outbreak of cholera devastated the region, leaving hundreds dead in its wake. Most of the town of Caborca succumbed to the epidemic.

A young Papago Indian lived in the village with relatives. When they died from the cholera, he was alone. He decided to pack his few belongings and walk to Gila City, a tiny settlement located where the Gila River enters the Colorado River not far from Yuma. There his tribe lived in a small encampment. As he walked out of Caborca, a young Mexican girl called to him. She was sitting in the shade of a low adobe house, crying. She told him her parents had died and she was alone. The boy invited her to accompany him to the Papago settlement.

For days the two walked across the arid desert and crossed the border into the United States a few miles west of Lukeville. The path they followed westward from the crossing was part of a road known as El Camino del Diablo, the Devil's Highway. This dry, windy, and waterless trace, where temperatures allegedly reached close to 150 degrees, had claimed the lives of thousands since the days of the California gold rush.

The few water holes in the area were known only to the Indians, and the young Papago knew where one of them was located.

The two travelers ran out of water long before crossing the border, and they quenched their thirst by sucking the juices from cactus fiber. It was bitter tasting, but better than nothing. At one point northwest of present-day Lukeville, the girl collapsed and told her companion she could go no farther. Feverish and dehydrated, he carried her to the shade of a low-growing ironwood tree and told her he would fetch water from a source farther up the trail. All night he hiked to the Tule Mountains. Late afternoon of the following day, he returned to the girl, carrying two large gourds filled with water.

For two days they rested. When the girl was strong enough, they continued their journey. They decided to walk at night when it was cooler. Around dawn of the following morning, they entered the low range of the Tule Mountains. Before noon, the Papago led the girl to the basin where he obtained water. It was, he told her, a place where members of his tribe paused during their journeys to rest and water themselves and their horses.

The Indian suggested they remain near the water for a few days. Here, he explained, they could refresh themselves, and game was plentiful. They cooked rabbits he snared and dined on a variety of abundant desert plants.

One evening, after they finished their meal, the Indian told the girl that not far from the basin was a place where his tribe obtained gold for making ornaments and utensils and for use in trading for goods at the white men's stores. There was more gold there, he said, than most white men believe exist in the entire world. She asked him to show her.

The next morning, the two hiked up a rugged canyon and eventually came out atop a granite ledge where they could look across a wide expanse of the desert. The Indian pointed to a location below in a narrow draw and told her the gold lay thick on the ground there. Together they scrambled down from the ridge and walked to the area he had indicated. They sat on the ground and picked gold nuggets as easily as picking flowers. Soon, the girl had gathered several fine specimens and tied them into her shawl.

When they were refreshed, they continued on their journey. They followed a trail until it came to a seldom-used wagon road. After many wearying days, they finally arrived at Gila City. Here, the boy and girl said goodbye to one another and parted ways. She moved in with a Mexican family and worked as a servant. The young Papago was never seen again.

The girl grew into a beautiful young woman and in time was courted by a local merchant named George Whistler. One day, she untied her shawl and showed him the gold nuggets it contained. Whistler grew excited and wanted to know where they had come from. She told him she found them near a secret water hole used by the Papago Indians far to the southeast. When he asked her if she would lead him to it, she refused. Whistler continued to court the girl and soon they were married.

Following the wedding, Mr. and Mrs. Whistler moved to Burkes Station, not far from Yuma. Whistler continued to pressure his wife into revealing the location of the gold nuggets, but she never wavered in her refusal. She once confided in a friend that she suspected Whistler had married her because of her knowledge of the gold, and she cursed herself for being such a fool. Still, they remained together, and she kept her secret to herself.

In spite of being married, Mrs. Whistler often received the attentions of other men. She was a beautiful woman and turned heads wherever she went. As the years passed, the story of her secret source of gold was well known to many in the region, and more men sought her in hopes of learning the location.

One was a handsome yet careless gentleman named Ventura Nuñez. Nuñez came to visit Mrs. Whistler when Mr. Whistler was at his place of business. Learning of this, Whistler confronted Nuñez one afternoon, and the two engaged in a heated argument. Before it was over, Nuñez pulled a revolver and shot Whistler, killing him instantly. Nuñez fled, but days later vigilantes caught up with him. He attempted to flee but was wounded in the leg and fell from his horse. Within the hour, he was hanged.

More years passed, and Mrs. Whistler confided her secret to a friend named Tom Childs. Childs was a well-known and highly respected citizen of that part of Arizona and a successful cattle rancher. He wrote down the directions to the gold precisely as she gave them to him:

Follow the wash up from the Tule Tank to a bench of granite rock. When you get to the top of the bench look in the bottom of the draw. You will see nuggets of gold in the creek bed.

Mrs. Whistler asked Childs to keep the location of the gold a secret as long as she was alive. If he ever found it, she requested that he give a portion of it to her two sons. He agreed to do so.

After Mrs. Whistler passed away, Childs made an attempt to find the gold of Tule Tank. He packed into the range and in a short time located the water-filled basin. For two days he ranged out from it, exploring one canyon after another in search of the one that led to a granite ledge overlooking the draw that contained the gold. It eluded him. Instead of one wash or canyon to follow, he discovered there were several to choose from. When he returned from his expedition, he told an acquaintance that he was convinced the gold was there, but because of the rugged nature of the environment and the numerous hazards, including rattlesnakes, heat, and thirst, he got discouraged. Childs also confessed that he lacked the stamina to climb around in those mountains.

A number of searchers have entered the rugged Tule Mountains to look for the lost gold. A significant percentage of them have failed to return, and weeks—even years—later, their bones have been encountered by subsequent hunters of the gold.

In 1957, a party of four men entered the Tule Mountains in a quest to find the mysterious draw where gold nuggets littered the ground. They had no luck, but as they made their way out of the mountain range, they came upon the bones of one who had gone before them. Among the scattered bones and rotted boots, belt, and camping gear, they found a small leather pouch. Opening it, they found a handful of gold nuggets.

Had the dead man found the draw? It would seem so.

Estrella
Mountain Gold

The Estrella Mountains lie southwest of Phoenix and adjacent to the Gila River Indian Reservation. Somewhere deep within this range is hidden a wealth of gold nuggets and dust, one that has tempted treasure hunters for over a century.

For generations, the Spanish mined gold and silver from rich sites throughout much of the American West, particularly Arizona. Many of the tributaries of the Gila River proved to be rich with placer gold, and it is estimated that millions of dollars worth of the ore was harvested by the Iberian conquerors long before Anglo settlers arrived in the area.

A successful miner named Ortega had grown wealthy extracting gold from several mines he owned and operated in Mexico's Sierra Madres. From time to time, he heard tales of the riches taken from sites in Arizona and decided to try his luck. After assembling a party including a mining engineer, two geologists, two hunters, a cook, two dozen Indian workers, and a string of twenty-five burros, he traveled north to the Gila River country to search for gold.

Ortega was a large man. He was fond of good foods and wine and considered each meal an opportunity to feast. His overindulgence over the years caused his weight to grow to three hundred pounds. When he traveled, it was in a wagon, for he had difficulty mounting a horse. During his journey northward into the Gila River country, Ortega rode in a custom-built wagon pulled by two stout horses. The back of the wagon was outfitted for sleeping. It was also packed with boxes of expensive foodstuffs and wine. Part of Ortega's travel preparations was always to include a cook.

On arriving at a village of Pima Indians south of the Gila River, Ortega made friends with the tribe, presenting them with gifts. In return, he requested information on the locations from which the Indians were known to harvest gold. To the Pimas, gold meant little beyond its rare use in making ornaments and jewelry, so it was a matter of small importance to them. They informed Ortega, however, that tribal tradition dictated that the source of the gold be kept secret from the whites. Ortega assured the tribal leaders that he respected their traditions and would give the matter no more thought. One evening, however, the miner invited one of the subchiefs to his wagon and offered him glass after glass of wine. The Indian manifested a keen desire for the wine Ortega selected. After two glasses, the miner told the Indian he would give him more if he would provide information on the Pima gold mines, including directions. Before the evening was completed, Ortega had the knowledge he wanted.

Days later, Ortega and his party, after crossing the Gila River, entered the Estrella Mountains. He hired a young Pima lad to take charge of the string of burros. Following the directions provided by the Indian, Ortega led them to a certain canyon, where they established a campsite. Three days later, one of Ortega's geologists found a thick vein of gold-laced quartz near the top of an adjacent ridge. At the same time, one of the workers spied gold nuggets in the stream that wound along the canyon floor and close to the Spaniards' camp.

As the miners dug the gold from the rock matrix and panned it from the stream, it was processed into ingots. In order to feed the party, the hunters set forth in search of game. Each day they returned with deer, turkey, rabbit, and other provisions. From time to time, a contingent would travel to the Pima village to trade for corn, squash, and beans, which the Indians grew on the plain adjacent to the river.

From the hides of the deer, men fashioned bags in which to store the nuggets and dust. As the weeks passed, the gold accumulated, and Ortega's dreams of growing wealthier than he already was were being realized. Each night, he slept with the bags of gold next to him, a weapon nearby to fend off any who might try to take it from him. Every morning he awoke and opened each bag to assure himself that the contents were intact. After several weeks of mining, he had accumulated thirty bags of nuggets and dust, and fifty gold ingots.

One afternoon, a hunter returned to camp and informed Ortega that he had spied a force of American cavalry. The troopers, he explained, appeared to be coming from Phoenix and would pass near the foothills of the Estrella Mountains.

Ortega had a fear of the U.S. Army. He had heard tales, many of them exaggerated, of their attacks on small villages of Mexicans and Spaniards. Ortega was concerned that the soldiers would learn of his gold and try to appropriate it. He fretted over what he should do.

The miner concluded that he must close his mine and send his men away. As for the accumulated gold, he would hide it in a place known only to him, and ride away in his wagon. When the threat of the American soldiers had passed, he would reassemble his men, return to the canyon, and resume operations.

Ortega ordered his workers to pack the gold onto the string of burros. He then sent them on ahead to establish a camp far south of the entrance to the canyon. He kept one of the workers to help him with the burros. He also retained the young Pima boy, who he placed in charge of leading the burros out of the canyon.

After allowing the main party sufficient time to leave the canyon, Ortega set out with his two helpers. Well before they were out of the canyon, however, Ortega directed the boy to lead the burros over to a shallow cave set in one wall. Ortega instructed the worker to unload the gold from the burros and carry it all to the back of the cave. This done, he instructed the boy to take the burros to the mouth of the canyon and wait for him there. As the worker toted the heavy bags of gold and the ingots into the cave, the boy led the burros away. Instead of taking them all the way to the lower end of the canyon, however, he stopped after sixty yards and allowed the animals to graze on some lush grasses that grew alongside the small stream.

With great difficulty, Ortega made his way into the cave. Near the back wall, he instructed the worker to dig a hole, place the gold inside, and refill it. An hour later, as the peon was refilling the hole, Ortega selected a fist-sized rock from the floor of the cave and delivered a series of mighty blows to the back of the man's head, crushing his skull. With a scream of agony, the mortally wounded worker fell atop the bags and bars. Panting with exertion, the corpulent Ortega pushed and shoved the body into the hole and refilled it. With that, he left the cave and, breathless, staggered over to his wagon. He clutched his chest as he sought to recover from his ordeal. After several attempts, he managed to climb aboard his wagon. After taking ten minutes to allow his breathing to return to normal, he hied the horses forward.

Moments later Ortega arrived in the midst of the burros, but the boy was nowhere to be seen. He called out several times but received no answer. Curious, but more concerned about surrounding himself with the safety of his party, Ortega proceeded on, nervous and fearful that he might encounter the contingent of American soldiers as he rode toward the campground of his men.

What Ortega could not have known was that the boy, after wondering about the decision to secrete the gold in the cave and watching the two men enter the cave, heard the cry of pain from the worker when he was struck. Fearing the worst, the boy fled.

It was sundown when Ortega arrived at the campsite. Agitated, he refused to answer questions about the gold. He waved away his dinner and, after consuming a bottle of wine, crawled into the back of his wagon to sleep. In the morning, as breakfast was cooking, one of the geologists carried a cup of coffee to the wagon. When Ortega did not respond to his greeting, the man walked away, presuming the *patron* was weary and needed his sleep. An hour later, the geologist knocked on the side of the wagon, and when Ortega did not respond, he looked inside. The big man lay there, fully clothed and unmoving. On investigation, the geologist discovered that he was dead, from an apparent heart attack.

Leaderless, the party held a meeting in order to determine what should be done. They decided to return to the canyon, retrieve the gold they were certain Ortega had left there, and go back to Mexico. On returning to the canyon, they spied a few of the burros, but no gold. They were unaware of the existence of the shallow cave that now contained Ortega's wealth. Dispirited, the group left the canyon and undertook the long journey home.

The Pima boy returned to his village and explained to the leaders what had happened. He was told that when greedy, evil men seek the precious metals that come from the earth, nothing positive ever occurs. The boy was instructed to put the events out of his mind and never speak of it to anyone.

For years, the story of the greedy Spaniard, his gold, and the killing of one of his workers was told among the Pima. The tale came to light during the early part of the twentieth century when a visitor to the village, a merchant, overheard it. When he pressed the Indians for details, they refused and spoke no more of it.

On his own, the merchant entered the Estrella Mountains in search of the lost gold hidden in the small cave. He returned empty-handed, but began making preparations for a second expedition. Weeks later, he returned to the range. He was never seen again. A story told around the area suggested that he was followed into the Estrellas by two Pima Indians on horseback. Both carried rifles.

If the story of Ortega's gold is true, and there is little to say it is not, more than one million dollars worth of gold nuggets and ingots lie buried in a small cave about midpoint in a remote canyon somewhere in the southern part of the Estrella Mountains.

The Lost Gold of the
Chocolate Mountains

The Chocolate Mountains lie about twenty-five miles north of Yuma where the Colorado River begins a half-circle bend in its flow toward that town. Today, Imperial Reservoir backs up the water of this river to a point just below the mountain range. Not far from one of the often dry tributaries of the Colorado River called Yuma Wash, an eccentric mine worker accidentally discovered and lost a rich deposit of gold that is still searched for today.

John Nummel was a reclusive prospector who explored much of southwestern Arizona near the Colorado River. He was born in Germany and, while a young man, migrated to the United States. After spending several months in unsatisfying jobs in New York City, he made his way westward to California to try to make his fortune in the goldfields. Having little success there, he left and settled for a time in Yuma. His prospecting expeditions took him northward into the Castle Dome, Trigo, Kofa, and Chocolate Mountain ranges. Never a man of means, Nummel, unable to purchase a burro or horse, walked everywhere he went and carried his supplies on his back.

When Nummel ran low on provisions, he would take a job at one of the mines in the area. Two of the most active mines were the Red Cloud and the La Fortuna. Nummel was not easy to get along with, and after a week or two at one of the mines, he would become argumentative with his foreman and quit. Strapping his pack onto his back, he would leave the Red Cloud and walk the forty miles to the La Fortuna Mine and work until he became impatient with his boss there. After leaving, he would return to the Red Cloud. Mine officials tolerated Nummel's eccentricities and short temper because he was a good worker. When he quit one mine, the officials assumed he would be back in a few weeks.

One day, Nummel, following an argument with the foreman, quit his job at the Red Cloud Mine and, after gathering his belongings, set out on foot across the desert to the La Fortuna. The path Nummel followed was an old Indian trail that wound through the foothills of the Chocolate Mountains.

As Nummel related his experience to a friend fifty years later, it was a hot day, and that part of the desert had very little vegetation. After crossing Yuma Wash and traveling for a few hundred yards, the prospector decided he needed a break and searched around for a bit of shade. He selected a narrow arroyo to explore in hopes of finding some. After several minutes of walking, he spied a palo verde tree near a low area where water gathered during the infrequent showers. Nummel sat down beneath it and leaned against the trunk, took a sip of water from his canteen, and as was his practice, examined the ledge a few feet away.

Running across the exposed formation was a vein of dark yellow quartz. Using his pick, he broke off a piece and turned it over several times in his hands. To his astonishment, the quartz was rich with gold ore. Rising from his position, he searched the area for more exposed veins, but found none. He checked to see if there were any claim markers in the vicinity and decided he was the only one who knew about this rich location.

Nummel reclined in the shade of the palo verde tree and pondered his options. It would be impossible for him to begin work digging into the vein and extracting the ore. For one thing, he did not have the proper tools. For another, he was almost out of food and water. In addition, during this time of year, temperatures near the ground reached 130 degrees, making for an uncomfortable situation.

Nummel considered returning to the Red Cloud Mine and making a plea for a grubstake, but he had so angered his employers that he did not think this a good idea. Instead, he decided to continue on toward the La Fortuna Mine and work there long enough to earn money to finance a return trip. He tucked the sample of gold-filled quartz into a pocket and set off.

Nummel filled his canteen from water holes he had located during previous hikes along the trail. A few days later, he arrived at the La Fortuna and was offered his old job. As usual, his temper got the best of him, and following another argument with his boss, he stalked away. The following morning he was hiking the trail back to the Red Cloud Mine. A few hours out of the La Fortuna, a wagon pulled by two horses came up behind Nummel. During the subsequent conversation, the prospector learned the rider was on his way to Yuma. On a whim, Nummel asked to ride with him. From Yuma, Nummel crossed the Colorado River into California and hitched another ride north to Picacho Landing, just south of the Red Cloud Mine and on the California side of the river. He arrived at the mine faster in this manner than if he had walked all the way from the La Fortuna.

Arriving at the Red Cloud, Nummel was surprised to find the beginnings of a small village nearby. One of the features of the young town was a saloon. Before approaching the Red Cloud Mine officials about getting his job back, Nummel stopped at the saloon. It was the beginning of a three-day binge, after which the prospector discovered he had spent all of the money he made at the La Fortuna.

After working for three weeks at the Red Cloud, Nummel quit, purchased some digging tools, and proceeded down the trail that would take him to his gold discovery. After crossing Yuma Wash, be began looking for landmarks that would direct him to the gold-filled quartz vein. In particular, he searched for the arroyo that led to the palo verde tree under which he had taken shade weeks earlier.

After an hour of hiking, Nummel determined that he must have passed the arroyo. He retraced his steps, ever diligent in his search. For the remainder of the day he walked back and forth along the trail, but could not find the arroyo. Now and then he would trek up one wash or another in hopes of finding the tree, but was unsuccessful. After two days of searching, he continued on to the La Fortuna Mine to find work.

Years passed, and Nummel continued to search for his elusive gold as he worked at the mines. During the 1920s, the Red Cloud Mine went out of business. Nummel was subsequently hired as a watchman to keep an eye on the buildings and property. When he was not patrolling the grounds, he set out on foot to try to find the gold he felt certain awaited rediscovery.

During the 1940s, an area miner named Clyde Stewart befriended Nummel and often gave him a ride when he found the man hiking alone on the remote roads. In 1947, Nummel was living on a meager state pension in a tiny shack near Laguna Dam, some five miles north of the Yuma city limits. Stewart would stop to visit the old prospector during his trips to the big town.

During such visits, Nummel invariably resorted to telling of his frustrations in trying to relocate the gold he had found years earlier up some remote arroyo. He told Stewart that it was between the crossing at Yuma Wash and the next water hole, a mile southeast of the gold vein.

On several occasions, Stewart, following Nummel's directions, tried to find the golden ledge. When he arrived in the general location, he found a rugged environment cut through with numerous washes and arroyos. It would take months, perhaps years, he determined, to locate the precise route Nummel took to the gold. After a number of fruitless searches, Stewart gave up. In 1948, Nummel had grown senile and was taken to the Pioneers Home at Prescott, where he died a short time later.

Today, the old Red Cloud Mine is a popular destination for gem hunters and rock hounds. For the most part, they collect the rare red wulfenite crystals found in abundance there.

There is an odd footnote to this story. In 1996, two men were hiking and camping in the southern part of the Chocolate Mountains. Having been to the old Red Cloud Mine several times and harvested the popular wulfenite crystals, they decided to see if the nearby Chocolate Mountains held any similar treasures.

After two days, they were nearing the end of their water supply and making their way back to a jeep they had parked near the mouth of an arroyo. As the two men made their way out of the mountains and into the foothills, they stopped to take a break in the shade of a palo verde tree. During their rest, one of them spied a ledge of yellow quartz nearby. Desiring to take a sample back to add to his collection, he knocked a fist-size chunk from the exposed vein.

Days later, when he had the time to do so, the hiker was sorting through his pack of rock samples when he came to the yellow quartz. On closer examination, he spotted a deeper yellow mineralization laced within. He took it to an expert and learned that the piece of quartz was rich with gold.

Several weeks later, the hiker and his companion returned to the region of the southern Chocolate Mountains to try to relocate the vein. Though they remained in the area for a week, they were unable to find it.

Just like John Nummel one hundred years earlier, the two men returned to the area several times in search of the gold vein, and as with the old prospector, it continued to elude them.

Now and then, someone who is familiar with the story of Nummel's lost gold will undertake a search for it; but more often than not, the harsh, rugged country proves to be too much for them.

W. C. JAMESON

Black Mesa
Gold Placer

Rock Springs, Arizona, is a small town located some fifty miles north of downtown Phoenix. A short distance to the northwest of Rock Springs lies Black Canyon, a rugged wilderness area through which flows Black Canyon Creek. During the late 1800s, prospectors found gold in Black Canyon Creek, and for a time, placer mining camps were established along its route. While the nuggets were of impressive size, and a few men earned small fortunes panning the gold, the mother lode was never found. In time, the creek was mined out and the camps abandoned. There exists some evidence, however, that the source of the gold in Black Canyon Creek lay near the top of a mesa west of the creek.

In 1901, two ranchers took some time away from their cattle and chores to enjoy a deer-hunting trip into Black Canyon. They spent several days in the gorge exploring by horseback. One afternoon found them close to the top of a broad mesa. From the summit, they could look down into Black Canyon. As they wandered about the edges and slopes of the mesa, they came upon evidence of a series of very old placer diggings in one of the drainages that flowed toward the creek. There were several locations where dry washing was evident, and the ranchers decided that, given the size of each, a significant amount of gold had likely been harvested from the area. The two men decided it might prove worthwhile to return to the area sometime and prospect for any gold that might remain. Determined to get on with their hunt, they rode away. As the years passed, however, the hard and continuous work of running their ranches kept them busy, and they forgot about their discovery.

Then one day in 1916, one of the ranchers was working in his barn when he heard the arrival of visitors. He went out to greet the newcomers and was surprised to find himself face to face with two old Mexican men leading a string of burros loaded down with mining and camping gear. The two men requested help regarding directions to Black Canyon. The rancher invited them to spend the night and sit down to dinner with his family. After turning the burros out to graze and washing up, the two men joined the rancher at the kitchen table. There, they told him their story.

The two old men—brothers, and both in their seventies—had walked all the way from some location deep in the Mexican state of Chihuahua. Their mother, who was ninety-two years old, had recently told them of an important discovery made by their father, who had passed away a few years earlier. As a young man during the 1840s, the father had arrived in the region of Black Canyon to try his luck at prospecting. During his stay, he found a rich placer field near the top of what he described as a high black mesa. After several weeks of dry washing the gold from the placer, he had exhausted his food supply and found precious little game in the area. Since he had accumulated enough gold to load down all six of his burros, he decided to leave. He left the Black Canyon area and made his way back to Mexico, where he and his family lived in relative luxury for many years.

The father seldom spoke of his gold discovery, revealing only the barest information to his wife. Just before he died in 1914, however, he called her to his bedside and told her as much as he could remember about the gold mine. With her help, he sketched a map showing the approximate location of the rich placer.

By the time the old man died, the gold he had brought back to Mexico decades earlier had long since gone for living expenses. The mother called her two sons together and, after urging them to go in search of the gold, turned their father's map over to them.

At this point in the telling, one of the brothers pulled a piece of crinkled paper from his jacket pocket and unrolled it on the table. It was the map prepared by the mother, and it depicted a high mesa flanked by numerous lower hills, all lying west of a winding stream. No roads were drawn, but it is likely none existed at the time of the father's visit to the area. Their mother told them the mine lay some forty miles north of a town called Phoenix.

As the two men spoke of their quest to find the location of gold found decades earlier by their father, the rancher was reminded of the old abandoned placer mines he and his friend had stumbled upon near the

W. C. JAMESON

summit of the black mesa. He refrained from saying anything, however, for he did not want to get the brothers' hopes up. Besides, he confessed in later years, he could not remember the exact location.

After spending two days with the rancher, the two Mexicans loaded their pack animals and headed toward Black Canyon. Leaving the ranch, they entered the rugged gorge. Given the rough condition of the terrain, and their age, they found the traveling difficult. Each evening found them so exhausted, they had little energy to prepare supper. It was all they could do to crawl into their bedrolls and fall asleep. After many days, they realized the map was useless. The depictions were inaccurate, and the distances and directions did not match the country through which they searched. The two men also admitted to themselves that they were too feeble and not prepared to continue the search. After two weeks, they decided to abandon their quest and return to Mexico and their mother.

More time passed, and many who entered Black Canyon found gold in abundance in the creek, as well as in several of its tributaries. When time permitted, the rancher himself traveled to the creek and panned for gold. As the years passed and he thought more and more about it, the rancher grew convinced that the old placer he once saw near the top of the mesa was likely located near the source of all or most of the gold found in Black Canyon Creek. He decided it was time to go in search of it.

The rancher attempted to enlist some acquaintances to join him in his effort, but all refused, claiming that the obligations of their own ranches kept them from doing so. Thus, he decided to go alone. Riding a horse and leading another packed with camping gear, he rode into Black Canyon and sought the trail that he remembered had taken him and his friend to the top of the mesa years earlier.

Luck was not with him. He explained later that he believed some of the watercourses he recalled from his previous trip had been altered, and that the landscape had changed as a result of landslides, forest fires, and other natural events. After a few days, his food supply ran low and he was forced to return home.

Though his expedition had ended in failure, the rancher was convinced more than ever that the site of the old abandoned placer near the top of the mesa was indeed close to the source of the gold. He was determined to continue his search, but the responsibilities of running his ranch kept him from it for years. More time passed, and he grew too old to go off on what amounted to dangerous expeditions into the rugged Black Canyon.

The rancher told a cousin about his discovery of the lost placer, and encouraged his kin to attempt to find it. The cousin outfitted himself for the trip and entered Black Canyon. He returned in a few days and explained that he had traveled through some of the roughest country he had ever seen. He had encountered steep cliffs, rockslides, impassable trails, rattlesnakes, and other difficulties. He described the canyon as "inaccessible."

A few hardy souls come to Black Canyon now and again to try their luck at panning gold from the stream. Some are successful, returning home with hundreds of dollars worth of gold as a reward for their efforts. Even fewer come in search of the little-known Lost Black Mesa Placer Gold, but they give up after only a short time, finding that the terrain is nearly impossible to traverse.

Black Canyon is a beautiful, fascinating geologic feature. Now and then, its wonders attract the rare fit and adventurous photographer or prospector. Its remoteness and inaccessibility, however, have combined to protect its source of gold from all who have entered thus far.

W. C. Jameson